Gurkha Reiver

WALKING THE SOUTHERN UPLAND WAY

Neil Griffiths

Cualann Press

ISBN 0 9544416 0 5

First Edition 2003

British Library Cataloguing in Publication Data. A catalogue record of this book is available at the British Library.

Printed by Bell & Bain, Glasgow

Published by Cualann Press Limited, 6 Corpach Drive, Dunfermline,
KY12 7XG Scotland
Tel/Fax 01383 733724
Email: cualann@btinternet.com
Website: www.cualann-scottish-books.co.uk

Biographical Note

Neil Griffiths is a former soldier and Fleet Street journalist. He has written for *The Guardian*, *The Scotsman*, *The Glasgow Herald*, *The Sunday Post*, *The Glasgow Evening Times*, *The Edinburgh Evening News* and many magazines. Griffiths is perhaps best known as the press officer for the Scottish Poppy Appeal, The Royal British Legion and the Gurkha Welfare Trust. He is editor of the Royal British Legion Scotland's journal, *The Scottish Legion News*.

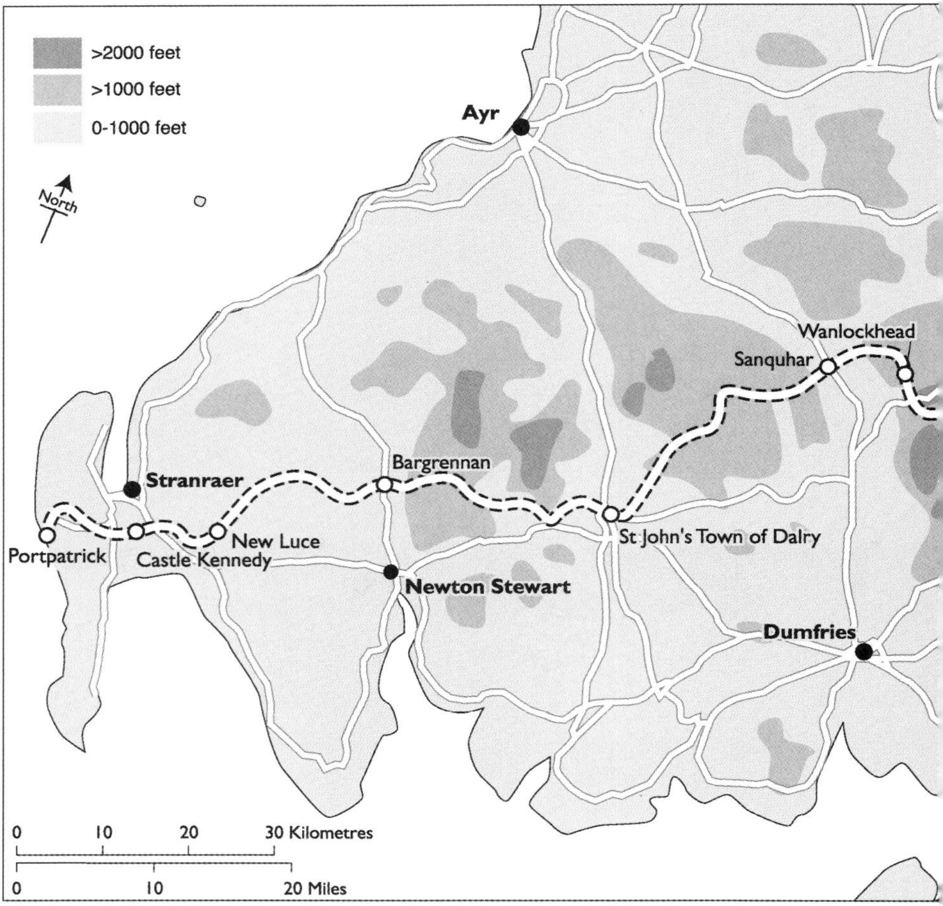
>2000 feet
>1000 feet
0-1000 feet
North
Ayr
Stranraer
Bargrennan
Wanlockhead
Sanquhar
Portpatrick
Castle Kennedy
New Luce
St John's Town of Dalry
Newton Stewart
Dumfries
0 10 20 30 Kilometres
0 10 20 Miles

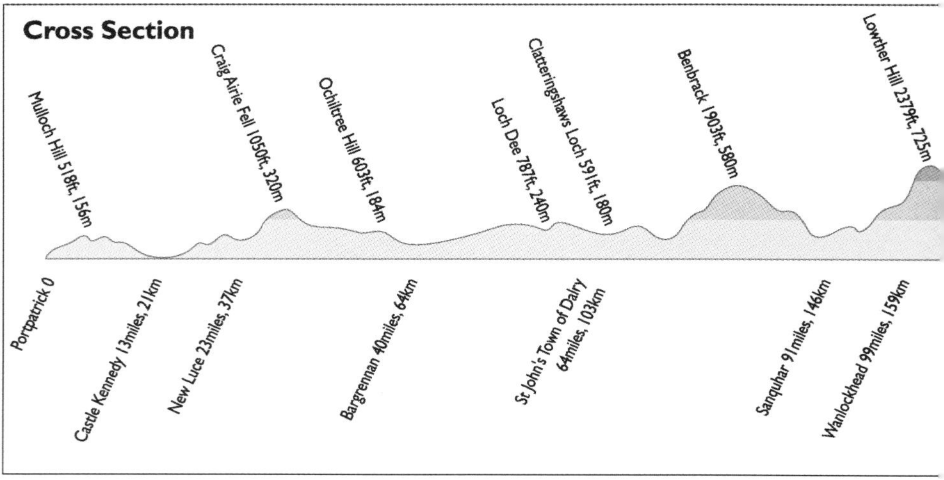
Cross Section
Mulloch Hill 518ft, 156m
Craig Airie Fell 1050ft, 320m
Ochiltree Hill 603ft, 184m
Loch Dee 787ft, 240m
Clatteringshaws Loch 591ft, 180m
Benbrack 1903ft, 580m
Lowther Hill 2379ft, 725m
Portpatrick 0
Castle Kennedy 13miles, 21km
New Luce 23miles, 37km
Bargrennan 40miles, 64km
St John's Town of Dalry 64miles, 103km
Sanquhar 91miles, 146km
Wanlockhead 99miles, 159km

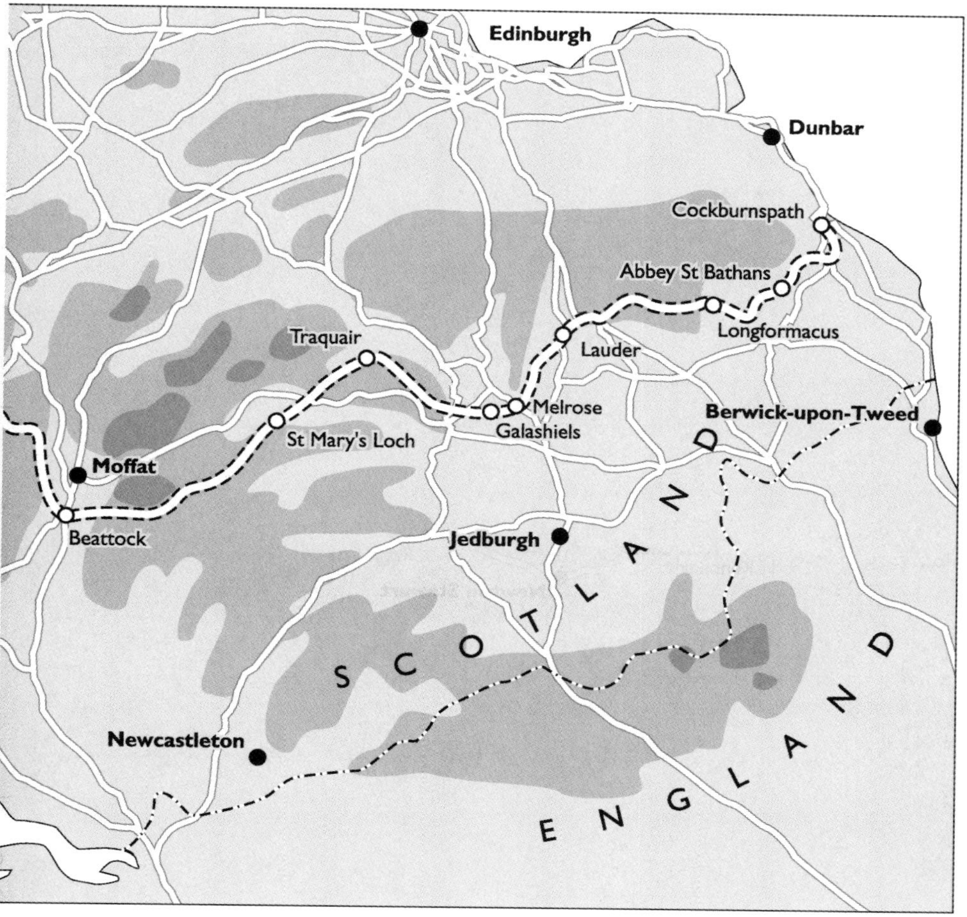
Edinburgh
Dunbar
Cockburnspath
Abbey St Bathans
Longformacus
Lauder
Traquair
Melrose
Galashiels
St Mary's Loch
Berwick-upon-Tweed
Moffat
Beattock
Jedburgh
SCOTLAND
Newcastleton
ENGLAND

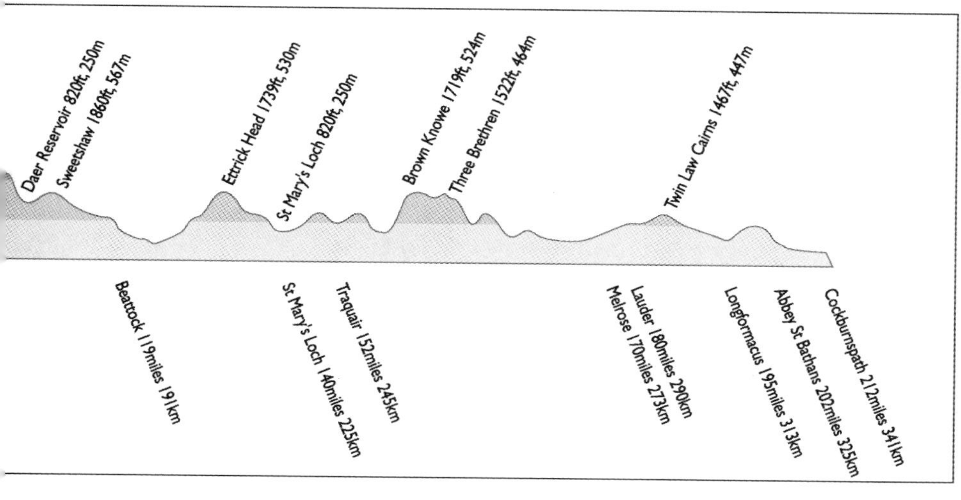
Daer Reservoir 820ft, 250m
Sweetshaw 1860ft, 567m
Ettrick Head 1739ft, 530m
St Mary's Loch 820ft, 250m
Brown Knowe 1719ft, 524m
Three Brethren 1522ft, 464m
Twin Law Cairns 1467ft, 447m
Beattock 119miles 191km
St Mary's Loch 140miles 225km
Traquair 152miles 245km
Lauder 180miles 290km
Melrose 170miles 273km
Longformacus 195miles 313km
Abbey St Bathans 202miles 325km
Cockburnspath 212miles 341km

Contents

Illustrations

** Gurkha Welfare Trust photos.*
All other photos by Neil Griffiths

Introduction

When envisaging a fundraising trek for the Gurkha Welfare Trust I had a mental image of a whole platoon of Gurkhas in full uniform, marching heroically across Scotland. Then the clouds cleared and focus became sharper. There would be a few problems with that scenario. No one would ever let me sign for thirty serving soldiers. Accommodating and feeding the men would tax even the slyest quartermaster, and I knew no one on the *Sunday Times* Rich List.

A brochure describing the Southern Upland Way with encouraging pictures of dry flat landscapes featuring young happy families skipping along well-maintained paths crossed my desk. The die was set.

Somehow four Gurkha friends were persuaded and – importantly – their commanding officers agreed to release them. With only a vague concept of the physical demands, I plunged into the organisational challenges with the same level of naïvety. None of what followed could have happened without the help of a lot of people – most of whom did not know me but the clarion call reached far further than I realised. Scotland's wish to help the wee men from the Himalayas was to prove both remarkable and moving in its substance and affection.

We were on the move for ten nights and the Royal British Legion Scotland either paid for or negotiated special B&B rates for nine. One member, Colonel Hugh Mackay of Twyndholm, paid all our costs at Newton Stewart. The Legion was also instrumental in organising publicity, from posters in neighbourhood shops to laying on receptions and the local press. They fed us too, and their appetite for Gurkha key-rings, tea towels and raffle tickets deserves a book of its own. Throughout Scotland the Legion branches raised over £6,000. I extend my humble thanks.

Over 3,000 ordinary Scots made donations, mostly of around £10 and were so unceasingly delighted to see us that I began to believe that my presence too was a cause for public rejoiing. Not quite true, but the generous part played by the Scottish people was the main ingredient in our success. Hats off to Scotland.

The critical but gentle advice given by my colleague, Leigh Howieson, a computer whiz and unpaid one-woman communications cell, made the difference between stumbling and striding. Thanks, Leigh. It is no wonder Gurkhas still ask after you and remain under the impression that I do no work at all.

Above all, this book is dedicated to the Gurkhas themselves, the hardiest, most loyal soldiers in military history. Legends. The trek was to teach me a lot about my own country but it was also an education as to the dignity and incomparable sense of fun to be found in these men, our oldest and best allies. If even a part of their extraordinary attributes are conveyed, then this book will have done its work.

Overleaf. Gyan addresses the crowd as Lady Stair rubs her eyes.

I

Portpatrick to New Luce

Lady Stair brought her hands together as if in prayer and ended her speech with the Hindu blessing: 'Ram, ram!' My four Gurkhas, Buddhists all, showed no surprise but smiled and clapped, joined by the fifty or so well-wishers that had gathered to see us off.

The group stood alongside the fog-shrouded harbour of Portpatrick, in Scotland's far south west – surprisingly, further south than Newcastle. This August Saturday we were ready to begin a march to somewhere called Cockburnspath, a village on the North Sea 340 kilometres that-a-way. It was cold. A group of supporters had turned out to wish us well, including the Deputy Lord Lieutenant, old soldiers, dogs, kids and, of course, the elderly and distinguished Lady Stair, who among other things was president of Stranraer's British Legion.

With four serving Gurkhas we hoped that the eight-and-a-half day walk would raise heaps of cash for the 12,000 surviving wartime Gurkhas who now live in penury back in Nepal. Proud in my red shirt with the crossed kukri crest, I also felt overweight and lumbering compared to my wee colleagues, who resembled dashing mushrooms under their broad-brimmed hats. They looked physically and mentally lively. I didn't.

It was my turn to address the crowd. Most of us are not good public speakers and I'm no exception. If there is one good maxim, it is: prepare beforehand. Not anticipating the great and good gathering in such numbers, if any at all, I, of course, had not prepared anything. There were no flowing words, no memorable phrases, just gratitude and a brief outline of what lay ahead: thin on words, heavy on hope.

Our senior Gurkha, Gyan, gave a quick follow-up speech. His solemn face, broken by flashes of white smile, told the crowd in simple terms how moved he was to see the good folk of Galloway and how his forebears, who had served Britain so faithfully, would appreciate today's donations back home in their Nepal hill villages.

Then, simply put, it was time to go, ditch the hats in the van, pull on the packs and start walking. It was exactly 9 a.m. but the moment was disappointingly ordinary. Planned for weeks, it should have been a culmination but instead it was merely another moment along the way. No trumpets. The unknown beckoned. Could I do it, would we gel, was I sane? Time to find out. I began walking like a lamb to the kebab shop.

As a group, we marched across the start line. Kali, his handsome high-cheeked features apparently irresistible to a group of ladies, was delayed as he kissed a line-up to happy high-pitched laughter.

Appropriately, the route went immediately upwards along the cliffs but we were stopped by a press photographer. 'Samachara sahib,' (newsman) I explained to grunts.

'I'm not fit enough,' I thought: 'But by God, I'm going to do this whatever, even if it's only pride that gets me through.' The onus of being in charge and setting an example would be a big stick too. Leadership is mostly about accepting responsibility, otherwise known as 'blame', while instilling confidence in your colleagues that everything is going swimmingly, really. The pretence of fitness would be a difficult one though, and 'acting' calm is a phrase containing more truth than I'd ever realised.

The Southern Upland Way is the UK's only official coast-to-coast walk. It cuts across the grain of the land. Every river en route runs north-south, except near the end, whereas we were to trudge almost due east, our steps taking a path corrugated with ridges and valleys. Don't be misled by the term 'Lowlands'. Here are the imposing Lowthers with Scotland's highest village, the Galloways and the rolling Lammermuirs. The subtle changes in culture, wildlife and topography every morning, would give us nine new landscapes for the next nine days. From forests in the west, to grassy uplands of the centre, to mixed farmlands of the east, the Southern Upland Way is one long department store of nature's offering. The larch-pole and sitka of Galloway transform into the beeches and elms of the Borders, giving an extraordinary education to the walker.

Even the geology changes with the accents. The dark grey wacke stone and soft cadences of Wigtownshire become the sandstone ribs and

Opposite: **Portpatrick. The team with our driver, Campbell McRoberts, pose for a pre-march picture.**

SOUTHERN UPLAND WAY

grittier voices of Berwickshire. In fact, the end is geologically linked to the Pennines, while the west shares its make-up with the earlier Cambrian mountains of Wales

This was, at the time, all stored knowledge, like a lost gold seam waiting to be re-discovered. No matter my forebodings, completion was the only option.

Two days before we left, Fordyce Maxwell, Farming Editor of *The Scotsman*, had phoned to say a friend had recently completed the Way and 'had nearly died'. Thanks, Fordyce. This brush with mortality was brought about, apparently, because of the miles and miles spent in forests 'that never seemed to end'. Monotony, however, didn't bother me. I was prepared for it and grateful that it wasn't something more serious.

Our walking had begun. Twenty-three miles of level countryside was a comforting prospect. The cliff route, still foggy, obscured what the brochures described as 'magnificent views' of Ulster, Kintyre and the Irish Sea's North Channel. Even the narrow inlets housed smoky curls. It was unexpectedly cold and silent. An hour earlier we had been ten miles away in bright warm sunshine but the group seemed comfortable and chatty while I began to blow like a thirty-cigarette-a-day man climbing up and down cliffs in the company of nonchalant men from the high Himalayas.

Sweat formed on my brow. This was not what the map had said. Didn't the website suggest 'family excursion' stuff? Behind me though came the sound of someone puffing. Brilliant! I'm not the only one finding this an effort! I turned round to see Kali looking back at me quizzically as he blew down the blocked barrel of a biro.

But suddenly we were on a road and not on a steep series of steps with chain bannisters. The sun appropriately broke through and the fogs in the inlets shrank symbolically. The track, due north until now, at last began to swerve east.

'There we go guys!' I shouted excitedly. 'Say goodbye to the sea. The next time we see it will be when we finish the trip!'

Unfortunately, a minute later we came across another inlet. 'Can I see the map?' grumbled Bishwa, at twenty-four our youngest member and usually the most silent.

'Never mind,' I thought. 'That's the last map-reading error possible.' It was about then that Gyan wondered aloud if there couldn't possibly be more than one map. Dhal grinned to himself at such obvious insubordination.

The land changed from a scuffed sea line to sweet cattle country and dark copses, but we saw no one. The HMSO maps were overlaid by one-kilometre squares but on a scale unfamiliar to us. At our briefing session the night before, with us sitting round in a caravan (great emphasis was laid on the perfection of our team), it had become clear that our first day would establish the great unknown. How much of the map could we cover comfortably in an hour or a day? How long could we stop for snacks and how often? How would contours, conditions underfoot and weather affect our progress?

None of this was obvious. Gurkhas famously switch from near grim passivity to peals of laughter but I knew from a cycle trip two years before that they never kept an eye on the clock.

This had confused me. How could these paragons of all that is military be apparently immune to that Army prerequisite, time? 'You can't rush Gurkhas,' said a retired British Gurkha officer, mysteriously. It took my sister to explain: 'If you're brought up at altitude, you do everything slowly.' Plus these guys had been raised in communities without clocks and watches. There's a considerable difference between a normal five minutes and a Gurkha five minutes. I knew this but appreciated from their history that when a Gurkha sees reason to move fast there is none swifter – ask anyone who has fought against them.

The landscape was tidy farmland with model railway neatness, its fields with an undulating order that rested easy on the eye, and all under a bright sun. At one corner I stopped to show the foursome where we were and how far we'd come, to stress the time factor and calculate lunch. This worked. Whether to stroll or stride would concern us for the next eight days.

Our steady pace was doing the business, albeit in uncompromising conditions. The guys were more interested in the adjacent standing stones.

'Ah Neil, this sundar chha,' (is beautiful) said Kali thoughtfully upon learning that they were perhaps 3,000 years old. The others nodded in

Overleaf. *Left:* **The Reivers exhibiting an unusually relaxed pace along the path past Stranraer.** *Right:* **Kali, corporal and char wallah.**

silent agreement. This part of Scotland is dotted with similar monuments, giving the area a unique spiritual feel, a daily reminder of how man had been here since antiquity and had worked the land since the Ice Age. The reverence the stones engendered among Gurkhas surprised me but perhaps as non-Christians they could easily associate with animism. Whatever, they instinctively understood the stones' symbolism, and as ancient places of worship, they were to be revered.

After crossing a low-lying heather bog and reaching the highest point of the Rhinns (the name for the hammer-head peninsular) in hot sunshine we could look down on the port of Stranraer, lying quietly, almost somnolent with a huge out-of-scale white ferry in the harbour. The neck of land here is only twenty metres above sea level. A little global warming would see the Rhinns as an island. A lane took us southwards before turning east again, the track hedged with honeysuckle and brambles. High summer with swallows, butterflies and hot cow muck! A daisy-dotted lawn in front of a picture-book farmhouse was ideal for a coffee break. Our first. My spirits rose as everyone sat down on the grass with sighs of contentment. This whole thing was working! Even the success of a pit stop was important.

Kali, Gyan and Dhal, oblivious to what experts may say about putting on a layer of clothing when stopping, tore off boots and socks to sit cross-legged while Dhal stripped to his shorts. When we're talking walking, Gurkhas are the experts, and I was not minded to comment.

While they could sit cross-legged with the nimble felicity of a lama, yours truly could only park his bum with big European legs splayed clumsily. In so many ways, I could never be like my friends.

Bishwa, as a mere rifleman, was easily the most junior. A member of the 2nd Royal Gurkha Rifles, he was currently serving with Corporal Kali in the Gurkha Demonstration Company at Sandhurst. Clearly, it was his job to make the milky tea that Gurkhas love. Kali asked courteously if I wanted some but I was already slurping coffee. It might seem an unnecessary question but the Gurkha wish to share should never be overlooked.

The British habit of reacting to a proffered slice of cake with: 'No, I mustn't. Really. Oh, go on then,' only baffles the Nepalese. The day before Kali had passed me a chip of apple on the blade of an ancient brown jackknife which I knew to take without fuss. Refusal is not polite.

We didn't talk much, contentedly absorbing the view, a green countryside squared by hedges placed with the thoughtful imagination of a dreamy child, whose artistry had included dog rose and yellow-flecked gorse. A herd of British Friesian came slowly up the road, the surface ringed with muddy hoof prints telling us that this was their regular route to the milking shed.

'We call these in Nepal 'Blighty gai' said Gyan (gai meaning cow), waving to the farmhands who seemed embarrassed but shyly returned his greetings. A startlingly beautiful blonde girl in her mid-teens sat upon a motor tricycle at the herd's rear. She, at least, wasn't shy and gave a cheerful wave. Our boys responded heartily. Clearly going to be the wicked woman heart-breaker of the Young Farmers set, if not already, I wondered.

Off again, and worried we'd spent too long resting (well, I was) the pace noticeably quickened. Gurkhas normally march at the apparently amphetamine-induced 140 paces per minute as compared to the normal British military speed of 116.

'When we finish tonight, let's march in to New Luce as a unit, with Dhal playing the pipes, doing Gurkha drill!' I suggested.

'But, Neil, you don't know our drill! Is very complicated. Few orders. No stamping. We should do British Army drill!' countered Kali.

'No,' said Gyan in his Staff Sergeant's voice, one accustomed to supporting officers. 'We should do it. Try, at least. Let's practise.'

I had baffled a retired Gurkha officer by asking: 'What's the Gurkhali for 'could you kindly step this way, please?' There was no literal translation. Gurkhali isn't that sophisticated. It was, I was told, only possible to order; 'Come here.' There is a 'please' word which could be added to soften things, but to make a civilized request requires the use of Nepali.

Having left the Army some twenty years before, it was surprising how little drill had been forgotten. Under a blue sky in a lonely rural lane, I did, however, discover Kali was right. It was practically impossible for an old dog like me to come to a halt or carry out any drill manoeuvre without a heavy military stamp, especially when told to stand at ease. There

Overleaf. ***Left:*** **Me at my most comfortable, sitting with a coffee.** ***Right:*** **Undressing for a coffee stop is a practice not favoured by the experts – but who was I to argue?**

were orders I'd never heard before but as a group we decided: we do it. Blame it on the sun.

At Portpatrick a healthy looking man in his sixties had crossed the road to wish us well. He was the chief executive of the Royal National Lifeboat Institution and was on a tour of inspection. He asked if we knew Gun Club Barracks in Hong Kong.

'Of course,' said Gyan, 'It was where every young Gurkha began his career from the end of the Seventies.'

'I was the commanding officer there in the mid-Seventies,' explained the other.

This was when we realised that the group had stumbled on two enormous coincidences; not only was this a former Commanding Officer of my regiment now based in Dorset, he lived 200 metres from Gyan's house. Spooky or what? Surely such splendid serendipity augured well?

'Lady Stair didn't know what a reiver was,' I thought aloud. 'Perhaps the name was a mistake and not enough people know a reiver was a Border plunderer of old? And what exactly does 'ram ram' mean?' I asked.

'Good golly, I suppose,' mused Gyan.

'Lady Stair's Close is an Edinburgh street,' I added

'Lady Stair is close?'

'No. No. A close in Scotland is a very narrow street. Lady Stair's Close is in Edinburgh's Old Town. Her husband, the late Earl of Stair, organized the funeral of King George V. Scots Guards, he was. It was his idea to have the four royal sons with heads bowed at each end of the coffin as it lay in state. At least, I think that was him.'

The foursome gave me a look of open-mouthed wonderment.

'Er, well, let's get moving,' I said, trying to change the subject in the likely event that I was utterly wrong. Later research proved this to be the case. The late Earl was indeed a Scots Guard but had, however, famously disputed the widely-held belief that it was the idea of Edward VIII that he and his royal brothers should mount the vigil on their late father in Westminster Hall. In fact, the suggestion came from the Duke of York, Colonel Scots Guards, and it was the Regimental Adjutant that had instructed them on the solemn drill. I should have known all this. I had edited the Earl of Stair's obituary, a fact I had nearly imparted with unbecoming cheerfulness to his widow that very morning when it first flashed through my head how I knew her.

Castle Kennedy, the Earl and Countess's country seat, gives its name to a charming village whose primary school saw us stop for lunch in its playground. My legs absorbed the sun's rays like those of an invalid put out on the lawn, perhaps in a wheelchair like Owen or Sassoon at Craiglockhart. There was some truth in this, of course. Pre-Way physical training had never exceeded two ten-mile walks on several weekends and the odd ten miles when the evening sunshine had been warm enough. My forty-three-year-old knees had flashed warning signals, necessitating the purchase of a first aid kit complete with knee supports (now happily stowed in Kali's rucksack). Attempts to jog to fitness had ended embarrassingly, when, after only a few minutes, I was so unsteady on my feet, passers-by assumed I needed help. My sweat ran more than I did.

Our party crossed the busy A75 (one of our so-called Euro Routes. Some of our aspirations are just so obvious. Can you see Germans calling the A75 a Euro Route?) to enter the magnificent avenue of two-hundred-year-old trees that colonnade the drive of Castle Kennedy, the stately home (not the village of the same name). Immense beeches, pines, oaks and even rhododendrons rustled high above.

I pointed to a bamboo bush as we passed a small loch: 'Bans?'

Again the giggles: 'No, bans is the full-grown bamboo.' The hilarity of misidentification aside, Gyan told me of the vast rhododendron jungles of Nepal which no local considered as beautiful, but as land appropriated and wasted by the invincible weed. From the depths of my cellar full of trivia I dredged up that the British rhodos come, not from Nepal, but from a Turkish or Persian genus – a fact I must have come across years ago, and whose triumphant moment had at last come. Its reception was, disappointingly, less than ecstatic.

Beyond the castle, past some monkey-puzzle trees, the route continues upwards towards a shelf-like escarpment, probably an ancient shoreline. There were several small kettle-hole lochs, a feature of the area, and two of them with crannogs, man-made islands dating from the Iron Age. Yes, Galloway is a special place.

'Do you know who Kali was?' asked Gyan slyly.

'Shiva's wife?' I replied.

Big grins. Kali looked momentarily embarrassed.

'Sometimes Kali can mean "black girl"', put in Dhal.

'Kaliketi,' (black girl) added Bishwa. I had wondered why Kali had a female name, especially that of the terrifying black goddess but knew that Nepalese names often appear illogical.

'My daughter's called Menees!' laughed Kali, by way of changing the conversation. 'It's Malay for sweet!'

Like most Gurkhas, these boys had seen the world. Whereas once they had never seen anything more sophisticated than a standpipe, they had now travelled the globe. The USA, Fiji and Hong Kong 'nor all its works' had not fazed them. Kali had been at the Jungle Battle School in Malaya where, among other things, he had stolen a name. Many Malay words appear in Gurkhali too, particularly for types of hills, synonyms of which the Nepalese can never have too many.

Our boots kicked up the dried mud as dust as we climbed the slope before coming upon a country house straight from a colour supplement, snuggled up to a group of beeches, as if for safety, beside a splashing stream. A tall elegant woman was standing by the front door, summer dress and tumbling blonde hair completing the picture. I couldn't resist calling out but the figure seemed momentarily taken aback – a woman's usual reaction to my openers, thought I, half peeved. 'My God, you're Gurkhas!' she exclaimed in pleasure. That's more like it. 'You must come in and join us for a drink!' Now that was even more like it! We took a split second to follow her into the back garden where a group of wealthy-looking types in their early sixties were sitting around a table. Every single male had one of those polished red faces that comes only with floppy hair and a heritable estate, or at least a commission in a good regiment, preferably the cavalry. The group, all linen and cottons, began pouring us iced squash as if this were for the summer edition of *Homes & Gardens*.

Presented as thrilling post-prandial entertainment laid on by the host, we shyly accepted – there was bags of time – and we could do with a drink, plus we might even get a donation. Our new friends couldn't have been more excited and even brought out cheque books. The mistress of the house, the tall blonde with a slight South African accent, had only lately returned from trekking in Nepal and produced the photos mounted on the distinctive Nepalese paper. A good-looking woman in her fifties, she seemed dismissive of her husband, gave the impression that she wasn't enjoying life here in darkest Wigtownshire, and that good days, like when Neil Griffiths and Gurkhas pop in for drinks, were rare.

Our boys, though, were the stars and that peculiar Scot-Gurkha mutual appreciation was abroad big time. Kicking myself that we had no badges or small gifts to give in return, I stuck a mental post-it note to shove something in my pack the next day. My presence was quizzed by one of the red-faces. I wasn't a former Gurkha, and had no direct links with Nepal. My answer, the one I'd given to the BBC a couple of days before, was that the situation in Nepal of the surviving wartime Gurkhas was a debt of honour which ought to be addressed and, happily, wasn't of the usual off-the-scale Third World dimensions. In fact, it was a problem which we could do something about and see the effects of our work.

I wanted to add that the prospect of a 200-mile walk through Scotland seemed pretty attractive too but couldn't admit it. I'd helped out on all sorts of fundraisers in the past. This one, I had decided, was mine to enjoy – and no, I'm never ever going to confess to any level of selfish pleasure whatsoever. The florid faces of our hosts beneath their straw hats blanked over: understandably, they wanted to meet a proper Gurkha: not some bloke from Edinburgh.

The love-in over, we hacked on over the dry hills through immobile cattle that eyed us with an uninhibited curiosity, like wide-eyed country children, and past dark silent copses until a plateau was reached where acres of white tree stumps, like bleached buffalo skulls, studded the grey landscape to the skyline. This was what used to be the Glenwham Moor. In the shimmering heat our back-up vehicle appeared unannounced with Campbell, our driver, and Mike, our host of last night and tonight, expressing delight at our progress.

'It was easy to find you!' said Campbell: 'We simply asked, "Seen any Gurkhas?"'

This, despite having seen almost no one, told me how observant were the locals; our movements were causing small blips on their radar. They were able, not just to spot and track us but also to identify and pass on the information. This wasn't empty countryside; it was one vast neighbourhood watch.

So, with progress noted, we headed off for the last stretch to New Luce where we'd reunite with Campbell and Mike.

Our pace was still steady, never relenting, only just this side of exhausting. There was a tendon-stretching rhythm to our legs, the type of pace best suited to nine days, I hoped. It begged the image of the boys walking for days as part of their youth. I recalled how one young corporal had once told me how his childhood had been spent traipsing 'one hour down the hill to school and then three hours back.' Wondering how demanding all this was to my colleagues, I was certain of one thing: it was not a stroll for me.

There is no Zen philosophy in walking, but there is a comfort and pleasure to be had, when one can take in the world and ruminate. But to us there was a reason above the idle foot-before-foot wandering of the normal hiker. The culmination of our efforts would put money in the pot for a group of forgotten old men. All the same, it is always a happy achievement to have walked from A to B. I don't know why, but the human spirit finds it uplifting and we were not immune to its joy. Incidentally, most Gurkhas cannot differentiate between the English words 'walking' and 'working'; we were combining the two for a better life for those we had never even met – but our hearts pumped for them with every step.

The pine forest's path gradually narrowed as if we'd walked into a spiky funnel, the edges thick, surprisingly, with clover. Eventually it was complete darkness, envelopingly warm, with only jungle-like shafts of blinding light. In fact, my friends always referred to woodland as 'jungle'. While Fountain Forestry's remit is big, it ain't that big.

Then, on the east side of Craig Airie Fell, it transformed into an airy broad-leafed wood of well-spaced ash and birch complete with sun-filled glades before we crossed the railway on a bridge opened by Lady Stair back in 1989. Her hand had a reach longer than we thought.

As we crossed a thickly tussocked field, Dhal, the only one from west Nepal, near Annapurna, suddenly imparted how surprised he was to have passed the agonising Gurkha selection course at the first attempt. 'I didn't think I'd pass. My parents were pleased. They had me late. An only child, so I was never spoiled.'

The logic baffled, especially as Dhal had several sisters, but the two of us walked side by side with the contentment that comes from completing a twenty-three-mile walk, his veins bulging over legs that would have credited a Himalayan postman. He was bigger than the others, his features, perversely, more like a Sherpa, and his English was excellent. Gyan, Kali and Bishwa came from the east, around Everest. Kali's mother tongue was practically Tibetan – and not, like the others, Indo-European based. (There are thirty indigenous languages among Nepal's nineteen million people). For Dhal to have walked into the Gurkhas, and the educationally stringent Queen's Gurkha Signals too, told me a lot. It was he who had learned to play the pipes, with the help of a short course at Edinburgh Castle, and had recently performed at the Queen Mum's 100th parade at Horse Guards. It's people like Dhal for whom the phrase 'don't underestimate' was coined.

The British Brigade of Gurkhas is massively over-subscribed where 20,000 selected men vie annually for the 230 places. To pass the physical alone, racing up a hillside with a *dhoko* (basket) full of stone on your back, it helps if you have Superman as a blood relative; it would literally kill some British recruits. These hill boys come from a warrior caste. Being a Gurkha is a calling, not an option, but becoming one has never been so difficult. My men had passed the most physically demanding entry test of any army in world history. To say that the Gurkha is merely a soldier is like describing Eric Clapton as a manual worker.

The thick green grass folded quietly under our tread. There hadn't been rain for weeks here and as a natural pessimist I reckoned that meant we were due a downpour soon. I was reminded of that old joke: what's the proper word for someone who goes around always bleating that it's going to rain tomorrow? Answer: a Scotsman.

The absence of tracks told us that no one had been this way that day, nor the previous day. Anticipating plenty of fellow walkers we even carried collection tins and Gurkha Welfare Trust stickers. At least we had the privacy to have a pee anywhere, I thought.

We marched into the village of New Luce with the full intention of making a complete exhibition of ourselves, pipes playing and our flying column of five causing a few hearts to flutter. But my hopes were dashed. Dhal took it upon himself to play a series of ludicrously slow numbers,

Overleaf. ***Left:*** **The same spirit: the boys of 1944.** ***Right:*** **The walk-trot that ate up the blurred miles.**

entirely inappropriate to a nation rejoicing at our heroic arrival. No matter what we said, or how we poked him, there was to be no variation on the dire medley of laments and dirges. Instead of an entrance marked by zip and dash with a toe-tapping heart-lifter, we came round the corner in slow motion as if in deepest mourning. People move faster at the Disabled Olympics. What should have taken less than a minute, took five.

The welcoming crowd, however, greeted us as if this were the Relief of Mafeking, with real pipes playing over the celebrations. We *were* heroes and the eventual drill manoeuvre of a 'Right Face' halt brought only cheerful laughter. You sods! New Luce was looking its best; the summer evening's sun was warm upon cosy stone cottages nearly hidden behind exploding flower boxes: a tourist brochure come to life. All the locals from neighbouring farms had turned out, including many with military ties and there was a table bearing – like a shimmering treasury – bottles of iced Becks. My usual British initial attempt at refusal dissolved in a moment, and I was irritated when a second wasn't offered with speed appropriate to my station as said heroic figure.

Despite their ready humour, Gurkhas are naturally respectful, even shy, and can be reserved in front of strangers. They grinned and nodded but with the exception of Gyan (a born PR man) were as unforthcoming as friendly Trappists. In short, they prefer to not talk the talk but to, literally, walk the walk.

For a few minutes, we basked in the atmosphere. The wee kids were excited and playing up, while ladies were telling (with no relevance at all) of their time in Egypt, and farmers were slapping backs with an agricultural catarrh-clearing strength. It was exactly the type of reception we wanted, complete with a collection for the Trust. We had everything except a seat.

The van took us to our B&B, a sprawling country cottage near Portpatrick, where our hosts Mike and Jean Rushworth lived with an immense Newfoundland dog. When Mike wasn't busy as chairman of Stranraer's British Legion, he was busy lighting up another cigarette: mostly, he was doing both. The dog was the size of a fully-grown boar but with the coat of a grizzly, hiding its famously webbed toes.

After a mile or so, I turned round to see that all my boys were fast asleep in the back of the vehicle. Yes, I'd become all possessive and proud. Being in charge normally means that when things foul up, it's your fault but today, the first day, everything had worked out. But God, my knees burned and we hadn't really gone very far: twenty-three miles in seven hours. Given the weather and absence of serious contours, perhaps we should, or I should, have hardly noticed any physical effects. But I did. I was surprisingly whacked on the most simple day of our walk. Perhaps it was the fresh air and sun. Things can only get, er, what? It was a mystery to me.

After a quiet evening, dining at a hotel in Portpatrick, perversely overlooking our starting point, with our hosts and support team, my body knew it had not been at a desk all day. A sunburned nose blazed the fact to every other diner. There had been the usual kerfuffle as to dress. It was strictly a night off but with only a dark suit in my luggage, I was stuck for choice. When this was discovered, a universal cry of horror went up as the lads rushed to change into blazers and regimental ties. 'Walking out dress', a term long-forgotten in the British Army, is still observed by the Brigade of Gurkhas, although it's called 'regimental mufti'. Everyone has a blazer complete with their unit's buttons. Dhal and Gyan wore the navy blue of the Queen's Gurkha Signals while Kali and Bishwa wore the rifle green of the infantry. It is an affront to wear anything other than a white shirt with these, as I once discovered when my failings as dhobi wallah (laundry man) led to the enforced use of blue shirts amid bitter mutterings of this not being 'proper mufti'. I blush still.

Tonight, if Neil was in a suit, they could not be seen in jeans. Only Campbell MacRoberts, unaware of this palaver, appeared in casual dress to a chagrined howl: 'Oh, I'm just the driver, aren't I? Just show me up, lads, I don't mind. Just a humble driver, that's me!'

Keith Halley, who had just retired from the Scottish Office as head of royal visits, was in charge of the finances and sale of Gurkha goods such as books, miniature kukris, teeshirts and teddy bears. Naturally he wore a suit.

Ah well, no one really fretted. In the bar our photos were taken about

Overleaf. *Left:* **Gurkha Pensioners, Lal Bahadur Thapa (left) aged 93 and little brother, Dil Bahadur, walk for ten days every three months to collect their pensions.** *Right:* **Still proud: another pensioner, Karna Bahadur Rana UC.**

ten times while Dhal was, understandably, making a close friend of the waitress.

Later I sat under the bright stars, the Milky Way clearly discernable, quietly smoking cigarettes with Campbell back at the cottage. Too wound up to go to bed, we cross-examined each other as to potential disasters. As leader, worry never quite disappears but I went to sleep utterly happy.

This Southern Upland Way could be leading somewhere.

II

New Luce to Bargrennan

That first morning we had started walking at 9 a.m., an hour later than planned, to accommodate well-wishers. While driving to Portpatrick along a country lane, a rabbit hopped ahead of us for two brainless miles before collapsing into the ditch with near terminal exhaustion like some dreadful omen. The gods couldn't have been more explicit. This, our second morning, we picked up the route at 8 a.m. and all of us felt, if not happy bunnies, then fresh and ready.

When we had arrived in Stranraer on Friday we had bought £80 worth of snacks at the local supermarket. The local press had featured our trip and passers-by were exuberantly generous. At the checkout, laden with chocolate, fruit, energy drinks and bottles of water, we were even slipped a £10 note. Outside Keith Halley and Mike Rushworth had run a stall all day to tremendous effect. Strangely, they hadn't sold much merchandise but were awash with donations.

Our packs were loaded with two bottles of water, energy drinks and a flask of boiling water. Food was to play a declining role as the trip wore on, as miniature Mars Bars, coffee and cigarettes usurped the too-solid and sensible sandwiches. Brain food or brawn food, that was the question – but we had to have drink.

Today's eighteen mile walk first took us across a plateau of rough grass mixed with thistle, spear plumes and hardheads, while the Land Rover track was sided by ancient sunken ditches, reached after a stiff climb past yet another pine plantation. On the New Luce-Bargrennan section much of the Way is on public and forest roads while the moorland areas are notoriously muddy. Guidebooks warn that in poor visibility there can be problems spotting the Way marking posts and that map-reading and compass skills may come into play.

In the distance came two figures moving in slow harmony, their bearing signalling fatigue from a mile away. At last, here were our first fellow walkers!

Their pace never wavered, with that head-down, slightly aimless step of the very weary that every soldier recognizes. Our group looked ridiculously fresh and spritely as we exchanged greetings in English.

'You're from Leeds?' I asked, detecting Mick Rushworth's accent.

Too tired to express surprise, they confirmed my guess. Having walked nearly two hundred miles, and nearing the end, their spirits should have been high. Instead there was the wide-eyed stagger of shipwreck survivors.

'How long have you taken? Which was the worst bit?' asked Gyan.

They were on their fourteenth day and, judging by the dull, sparse replies, nearly every day had been the worst. The guidebooks state that the absolute minimum for the Way is twelve days; we were planning it in eight and a half. Just how crazily optimistic had been my planning? We moved on; my apprehension returned. I recalled a Gurkha officer chuckling over some of my routes for the latter stages and how he would like to see us cover the distances in the time given. To hell with it! Too late to worry now, I thought, dismissing experience and expertise in one.

Progress remained steady and we stopped for hot drinks in a hillside hollow. The humid air and low sky stirred the area's insect life to investigate, not just the surrounding sheep muck, but also the visitors from Nepal and their Scottish colleague.

Bishwa settled down on the grass with flask and cups before pouring out the coffee. While on the phone, I interrupted: 'Bishwa! Don't make coffee with your bare hands! Use a teaspoon!' I fumbled for the spoon in a side pocket of my shorts before tossing it across, only to see it land neatly in some soft sheep shite. He uttered a grave 'Oh!' picked it up, and with only a quick wipe plunged it into the coffee jar. My reaction was as if a hornet had just disappeared up my trousers.

The sweep of the countryside spoke of heavy glaciation, low and rounded where summits assume an importance way above their actual height. Nevertheless, we were slowly climbing, and heading ever north-east. Place names, like Knockatoul, were nearly all Gaelic, a rarity in the east, which told us again of a departed culture. The Saxon names of Nithsdale, Clydesdale and Annandale lay ahead of us.

As we ambled, the grass became short and scabby with thistles and yarrow, but on our left was a long dry-stane dyke offering protection to ragged gorse, in which Dhal had noticed something hidden to my eyes.

'Here, Neil, look,' he said quietly, half hunched and padding towards the bushes. 'There!' he grinned mischievously, pointing with his thumb. Suddenly I could see it, the side view of a hen pheasant eyeing me like a kid caught in the pantry and rather hoping that I hadn't seen her. I was baffled. How had Dhal seen the bird from so far away? Answer: his eyes could spot and interpret movement in a way unknown to me. Like a true hill boy, he was much closer to nature than I would ever be, and it showed.

The sun pushed through midmorning as we entered another forest and half trotted down an immense sunlit firebreak of long white grass where the smell of drying conifer filled our lungs. The map showed this sprawling collection of plantations would take at least an hour to cross – one of those 'unending' ones we'd been warned about which threaten sanity. I doubt, however, if I'd ever had such a glorious Sunday morning. The Way crosses the Mulniegarroch on a neat little bridge and leads to the ruins of Laggangairn (meaning hollow of the cairns) after passing a tall pale-wood beehive-shaped overnight shelter. This comes as a total surprise to the walker as it is not only so far from anything but looks totally out of place.

The Laggangairn Standing Stones are grouped in a woodland clearing as if in conclave. The route is coincidentally on the early Christian one to St Ninian's shrine at Whithorn but the man-size monoliths radiate a quiet spirituality of an earlier and lost religion which the Reivers seemed to pick up as we stood in silence.

'Neil, please give me change,' asked Kali quietly. I handed over some coins which he placed on the stones, hands momentarily clasped in prayer before a graceful and swift raising of the arms. The action seemed so entirely appropriate that as we left, I, too, felt blessed.

The monoliths predate Scotland as a Gaelic country. They have stood here since before the Scots crossed the sea from Ireland. The Picts left us few clues but these were some of them. No wonder the phrase 'memorial in stone' has such eternal resonance. It occurred to me why the Galloway map bore so many Gaelic names, while those of the Borders did not. The Gaels had swept through here from Ireland to Argyll (Ar-Gael, Kingdom of the Gaels) and on to the Highlands. Those who had remained here were known as Gallgaels, I remembered from some childhood school class. The

East, with its thorpes and dales, was Saxon and Old English. The ancient Northumbrian kingdom of Bernicia stretched as far north as the Forth. Our Pictish forebears had, however, disappeared like wraiths in the mist of history. I suddenly understood all this in an almost supernatural flash that was part exciting and part disturbing.

The Picts, like the North American Indians, worshipped the spirits, which resided only in trees, rivers and lochs. Living in a time when so much was unexplained, there was at least one certainty: stone outlived us all. That was clear.

I didn't know then that the Himalayas are studded with ancient Buddhist chortens, stone religious monuments, and sometimes called *stupa*. Buddha himself, don't forget, was born in Nepal. Also there are Mani stones which are small and flat, meticulously carved with Sanskrit and are piled to form long, low walls. These you always pass on the left. There was, then, unbeknown to me, a further link between our cultures.

Further down the firebreak we passed another English couple, a tough looking bloke and a girl with an immense bust. 'Genuinely outstanding,' I thought to myself. We'd seen them (the man and woman, that is) up ahead and had used them as a useful impetus to speed up and overtake. There were warm murmurs of approval at the sight of a woman bearing a large pack. The introduction of this Nepalese custom was clearly a sign of civilisation and to be welcomed. But they'd put on speed themselves, as if grimly determined to hold on to the lead. Usually, after a show of spirit, the overtaken suddenly fade lamely, but not these two. We couldn't understand it, but to show good feeling, Gyan grinned round at the busty girl and uttered the memorable: 'Big boots, eh?'

His look of panic when it was realised she'd misheard will stay in the annals of Gurkha history forever. Gyan and I, at least in this respect, even if subconsciously, obviously thought along the same lines.

The Way crossed the Tarf Water and entered the mature Killgallioch Forest where fellers had been at work and the air was filled with the evocative tang of pine sap. Lunch was atop a cleared hill, Craig Airie Fell, with the forest below us, and a huge view behind with moorland reaching

Opposite: **Belted Galloway: the finest beef cattle in the land.**

from Ireland to the Solway, dappled by small white clouds floating across a celestial blue sky. Our pace had been break-neck and I needed a spot of idleness. Coffee and cigarettes made it 'very heaven'.

Cameras and phones came out. Dhal had climbed onto the trig point and removed his cap to take in the view. It was here I took a snap, with Gyan and Kali sitting with Dhal towering over them, that best encapsulated the day, if not the trip. Dhal looks as if he's on Kali's shoulders and the background is of small fluffy clouds set against a dreamy azure. It was to appear in many magazines, even *The Scotsman*.

Partly because blue and white are the Buddhist colours, I was reminded of Lama Govinda's *The Way of the White Clouds*:

> *Just as a white summer cloud, in harmony with heaven and earth freely floats in the blue sky from horizon to horizon, following the breath of the atmosphere – in the same way the pilgrim abandons himself to the breath of a greater life that leads him beyond the farthest horizons to an aim which is already present within him, though yet hidden from his sight.*

It was appropriate that a Buddhist tract should come to mind: there was a stillness and beauty which would have suited meditation. The view, too, was a heart-lifting affirmation of life itself. From our vantage point, the glittering sea was visible to our west and far south, representing the past, while to the east, our route, the future, threaded its way unseen to the skyline and beyond.

'This, Neil, is a gunong,' explained Gyan. 'A hill with trees around it but none on top.' I recognized the word as Malay; it was used in jungle warfare for parachute drops, and similarly, a *ladang*, a cultivation in the jungle. Gurkhas have more words for hills than Eskimos have for snow. Normally I stuck to the normal word for hill, *pahad*, and allowed Gurkhas to interpret exactly what I meant. If I got too exact, it might be taken literally – and wrong.

This stop was a full fifty minutes, by far the longest we were to take. A Sunday lunch laziness overcame us and the near sleepy reluctance to

***Opposite:* My favourite picture. Dhal atop Craig Airie Fell trig point, Galloway.**

GURKHA REIVER

leave was only overcome by the sheer necessity of getting into town for supper. The forest road below was broad and stony as it wound past more kettle-hole lochs and countless Gaelic place names. The Bal prefix, town or village, as in Balmurray, was the most common, while the cutest was Tannylaggie, meaning meadow hollow.

When Bishwa and I strode out of the forest it was to witness a small herd of those magnificent cattle, the belted Galloway, known throughout the world wherever beef farmers gather, and familiar to the rest of us for its sturdy black body with a broad white band round its middle. A sort of art deco cow, its body is practically box-shaped, capable of surviving on the most meagre of grazings. It is a bonny animal, the only cow ever made into a cuddly toy (both my sisters had a Billy Beltie, and they grew up well adjusted and successful – the girls, that is) and is a proud symbol of the area's heritage. Not many know that Blue Grey cattle are a cross between Shorthorn bulls and Galloway cows. This information arms you for every known social occasion. Go forth and impress. I took a photo of one handsome specimen in profile, realising later that I should have included the fascinated Bishwa.

As we marched over a tiny burn I realised with a jolt that it was the Bladnoch, a name from my childhood. My father was brought up near here, by an aunt and grandmother at Wigtown, less than twenty miles away. I had fished the Bladnoch as a boy. It was where, aged eight, I caught my first salmon, albeit a fry, and my first trout, its stomach filled with whey gobbled up from the now defunct Bladnoch Creamery. In the immediate post-war years my father fished it with neighbour and film star James Robertson Justice when the two of them would arrive in the actor's Rolls Royce filled with unwashed Labradors. Justice's cast was the longest my father has ever seen.

In the mid-eighties the Wigtown house had been sold, after a century's ownership, and the aunt moved to a cottage in the village of Bladnoch, three miles away. She, along with many of my father's side, now lies buried in the Wigtown cemetery, a graveyard made famous by Covenanters, the Wigtown Martyrs. The Martyrs were executed by drowning. Tied to posts at low tide in Wigtown Bay, the sea rose to claim them. And here I was, my stride across the Bladnoch a link with the past. As a child I had rarely lived in the UK and never in Scotland but the

Wigtown farmhouse and estate had been a touchstone of continuity. The family holidayed there at least once a year. Part of my father's family, the McGeochs, had lived here for perhaps a thousand years. Their name comes only from Wigtownshire.

The First World War had a convulsive effect on Scotland, which even now is more than a dim folk memory. As a boy it seemed quite normal to me that a rural village was full of single old ladies: Miss McKinna, Miss Smith, the Misses Todd, Miss McGeoch; the list went on and on. Wigtown, it seemed, was full of daft old bats that drove Morris Minors like crazy and gardened until the day they could no longer rise from their frail knees. In the sixties, it was sadly all too normal for Scottish villages to be filled with spinsters. I was a teenager before I realised that so many lost their fiancés in the Great War.

The forest continued, our horizons hemmed with cool dank smells and the muffled tramp of boots on road. At last, we came to a small patch of open country with blazing sun on bright green grass. A group of farm buildings, unusually of brick, were formed around a silent yard but adjacent was a residential caravan adorned with a flap of cardboard, announcing 'Teas and Lemonades' in thin felt pen. A series of small tree stumps, shaped into stools around a chunky table, beckoned. The decision was unanimous and unspoken; we threw ourselves down on the grass around them.

I half expected a farmer's wife to come running, dusting flour from her apron, crying 'Lawks, it's they Gurkhas' (yeah, okay, it was a hot day and I was tired) but instead, a newly-retired couple ambled from the caravan to take our orders.

'We knew you'd come,' smiled the husband. 'Read about you in the papers.'

Impressed that they knew our movements before we did, we were further delighted when piping hot tea along with a jug of iced lemonade arrived. This was living!

A few days before we had visited a 'Gurkha' restaurant in Edinburgh

Overleaf. ***Left:*** **Some of the route was overgrown. Here Dhal, just east of Bargrennan, wishes for a kukri to clear the way.** ***Right:*** **Miles to go but Galloway was a joy to walk through. This picture convinced me that I look a prat in a baseball cap. Until then I thought I was George Clooney!**

which was decorated with pictures and memorabilia of Bishwa's old regiment, the 10th Gurkha Rifles. To our surprise, and their embarrassment, our hosts had to admit they had never served, and weren't even hill men but came from the Kathmandu valley. They were much darker than our boys. Given the animosity between those of the high Himalayas and the lowlanders, I was relieved and pleased that our visit was marked by a 10% discount and free beer. In fact, the evening was such a happy occasion and the food so delicious, we were due a return visit. Tables, in short, were not turned over and neither were we.

My vocabulary was on the increase. Nepali menus state 'hen', *kukhura*, not 'chicken.' I explained the Scots faintly comic habit of addressing friends as 'hen' as in 'How are you, hen?' '*Kasta chha, kukhura?*' Or simply 'Hello, hen!' '*Namaste, kukhura!*' This local knowledge was received with rapturous glee, and not a little incredulity, to the point where Dhal and Kali took to using it to greet complete strangers – albeit completely attractive female strangers – to hoots of laughter. It was a great opener or ice breaker.

As we sat in the Galloway sun, a plump Rhode Island Red came carefully stepping round the corner, in that careful hen way, as if partly lost in thought.

'Namaste, kukhura!' I pointed. The Reivers laughed and laughed like we'd been hit by a cloud of nitrous oxide. The moment was re-lived for the next week.

Our hosts, apart from their second sight, proved an interesting couple. 'We're members of the British Legion too,' they told me after hearing that one of my jobs was as its press officer. 'Of the Malaga Branch. We only spend summers here. In fact we both sponsor Gurkha pensioners through the Gurkha Welfare Trust.' There was, of course, no charge for the refreshments. 'Look upon it as a donation.'

As we hit the road again, our busty English girl and her man entered the yard but it was with genuine warmth that we greeted each other. No mention of the misunderstanding was made which possibly meant the original message had sunk in or that the comradeship of the Way had meant the incident was a closed book.

Our destination required three hours of rapid movement, and at one point the route closed in to see us battling through head-high bracken, which not only told us how rarely the path was used but prompted wishful cries for a *kukri*.

The famous kukri engenders immense pride and nothing else so succinctly says ‘Gurkha.’ The crossed kukri appears on all Gurkha paraphernalia, from cap badges to unit crests, from stationery to shoulder flashes and cannot be mistaken for any other part of the British Army.

Although the Gurkhas departed early from native dress and adopted a European style of uniform, they never gave up their traditional fighting knife. Designed for cutting, as opposed to thrusting, it is seventeen inches overall with a blade of about eleven inches. The scabbard has a metal chape (pointy bit on the end) and leather frog, while a small knife and honing steel are tucked into the back (and fall out all too easily). Gurkhas are so comfortable with a kukri in their hands that they tend to prefer them to firearms which, in any other unit, would be a serious offence, but when you see what they can do with the kukri, you don’t want to get in their way.

Gurkhas use their knife for almost everything, from gathering firewood to erecting fences. I have one whose handle has clearly taken a hell of a hammering at some stage. For many years British troops were led to believe that the kukri could be used as a boomerang too. The concept ignores the rules of aerodynamics but has a sort of wonderful comic element.

The kukri doesn’t have the pitiless beauty of a samurai sword. Instead it possesses a hardy working earthiness, but no matter how you look at it, as a tool, an ornament or a weapon, the kukri speaks of violence, of blade on bone, hot blood splashing and chopped throats. Surprisingly, it takes the feminine gender which perhaps reflects a man’s regard for his first protector.

The nonsense about a drawn kukri being required to draw blood before re-sheathing is laughable too. Daily kukri inspection alone would be a blood bath. Furthermore, on operations, particularly in jungle warfare, Gurkhas like to hold a kukri in one hand like a RoboCop extension. Anyone who believes that drawing blood for unexplained spiritual reasons in a jungle-sore environment doesn’t know the Gurkhas. Pragmatism is a Gurkha characteristic where religious observation is readily dumped if it conflicts with military requirements. Hence our boys eat whatever they like while in the Army. Their society honours warriors, especially live victorious ones. Nevertheless, old soldiers swear blind they have witnessed the practice and I don't doubt them. They just don't appreciate the droll Gurkha sense of humour and that they'd been wound up. It is, however, vital, with the knife worn on the right buttock, that you remember it when sitting down.

Prior to our departure from Edinburgh the lads felt it necessary to present the City's Lord Provost with a ceremonial kukri in a dazzling silver scabbard decorated with peacocks. Eric Milligan had been deeply moved by the occasion, held in front of the City Chambers on the Royal Mile.

'You are the Queen's representative in the capital of Scotland,' explained Gyan, meaning that the Lord Provost was also the Lord Lieutenant, 'and we wish to make our thanks to the people of Scotland through you.' Eric gave a heart-felt speech about the debt Britain owes the Gurkhas while press snappers clicked away. The boys were in their broad-brimmed hats and made a fine picture. Politicians had little to lose by associating themselves with our walk, but Eric was genuine in his gratitude and donated generously.

I'd phoned Jackie Bird, a well-known Scottish BBC TV presenter, to ask if she could attend, but she'd laughingly accused me of scraping the bottom of the barrel and anyway she would be working. Jackie, too, has a long record of helping the ex-Service community and had even presented, gratis, a five-minute Poppy appeal broadcast that I had written and directed. She visited an old soldier's home in Glasgow into the bargain. On that occasion the taxi to whisk her back to the BBC studio didn't turn up and both of us had several minutes of panic before I could hail a passing cab.

When I dropped her off at Queen Margaret Drive the cabbie asked: 'That that Bird aff ra telly?' On the other hand, he might have meant 'that bird'– either way, he was right.

The remainder of the day's walk was downhill through open moorland to the hamlet created for forestry workers at Bargrennan on the River Cree. There was a moment to take in the view from the trig point at the Hill of Ochiltree which was, at 184 metres, not very high but gave a wonderful panoramic view. There was Loch Ochiltree to the west while the massive forest of Glen Trool – tomorrow's route – spread itself across the eastern horizon like an immense dark green blanket. The last part of every day, despite better instincts, saw my pace accelerate uncontrollably. Call it the horse wanting to get home syndrome or a deeper part of me that felt obliged to lead at the end but there was always a near psychotic urge to gallop to the finish. Part of it was certainly a wish to get everything out of the way as soon as my little legs could make it but, whatever the cause, it hurt. Bordering on neurosis, I was never able to stroll the last hour. I ought to write a paper on the condition, really I ought. Arriving first at the pick-up vehicle, parked beside the River Cree, I was proud to wish the men a hearty '*Shyabash*' (well done), as they charged in behind. Campbell was, of course, standing beside the van like some tournament official, grinning in the sun.

Tonight was another night off, I thought, as I eased my creaking knees from the vehicle outside our hotel, Newton Stewart's Galloway Arms – an establishment whose fabled comfort I had known of in my youth. Nowadays, I was told by the former Gurkha officer who had kindly footed our bill, things were very much a tale of faded glory, a story applicable to the whole area whose big century had begun in 1800. In those days, before Wigtown harbour silted up, Galloway farmers could even send their fatstock direct to Liverpool and Manchester.

Scotland's south-west had once been a wealthy area. Hence Wigtown's huge town hall; it had anticipated only growth. Dumfries & Galloway remains a contented part of the world, level-headed and not given to frippery. D&G hereabouts, for instance, does not stand for Dolce & Gabana.

We enjoyed a couple of lagers in the hotel's beer garden, surrounded by roses as the summer's evening fell cold. Kali delivered increasingly preposterous stories about his military achievements while we tried not to laugh. The moment was too frequently interrupted by the traditional Scottish drunk, ex-soldier department, and unavoidable hazard of wherever two or more are gathered together for a drink anywhere in Scotland. Does every village have one? The type with bad teeth, bad skin, short of stature and short of practically everything else including IQ, manners and the capacity to string a whole sentence together. One particular nuisance was a former King's Own Scottish Borderer who wouldn't go away, demanding that we hear him out. I've worked all over the globe and never had to face the threat of itinerant drunkard as a routine peril. What's wrong with us? Our guys simply sat there, bewildered and embarrassed, not knowing what to do. Campbell looked frozen, begging in a whisper not to mention that he himself was ex-KOSB.

The new owner was eager to please and even served Kali and Bishwa with a rice dish not on the menu. Only recently purchased, I wondered if the property would ever bring a return. The next morning breakfast was in a dowdy room which I could recall as once the scene of grand family lunches with white linen and lit candles.

It was during supper though, in tired reverie, that two pensioners in British Legion blazers appeared, their lapels flashing with badges. I admit it: my heart fell. Having written to the Newton Stewart branch of the Legion and receiving no offer of help whatsoever, not even advice, in short, no reply, I was nettled to have my eyes fall upon this twosome. Keith and Campbell had spent the day managing our stall right next to the hotel with only small success. Admittedly it was a Sunday but they'd worked hard and done the business. Now we had two chancers upon our doorstep who had ignored all our letters and pleas for assistance. They couldn't lie their way out of it. Just by being there in the hotel proved that they had received my letters.

The team was not ready to accept offers of drinks until midnight. We were too tired, but were obliged to listen to their stories. And boy, could they talk. The greeting that we had been utter fools to set up our stall beside the hotel instead of the newly-opened supermarket 'which had a very busy day today' was particularly irritating.

Of course, we were too polite for physical violence, but they were perplexed as to why we didn't want a drinking session with their wonderful selves. One of them recounted that he, personally, had paid the £14 for the town's poppy wreath last Remembrance Sunday and could I do anything about this terrible iniquity.

I later crawled into bed, swearing blind I'd kill the next boozy bore who crossed our path, preferably with one downward swipe of a well-oiled kukri.

Opposite: **Edinburgh's Lord Provost, the Rt Hon Eric Milligan, with presentation kukri and special bodyguard**

III

Bargrennan to St John's Town of Dalry

~~~

The van emptied us on the western edge of the Glen Trool forest, at the Middle Bridge of Cree, in wet drizzle. Clad in what the catalogue called 'Forest Green' waterproofs with white crossed kukris on our left breast, we padded through the mature pines and newly-planted areas along sodden gritty forestry roads, avoiding spattering puddles. Gyan had, unbelievably, produced a ladies' umbrella and grinned gamely at the ribald comments. Had he no shame? Our heads were only protected from the downpour by baseball caps bearing embroidered kukris. We saw the world under dripping grey suede peaks.

Much of our twenty-two mile third day would be in the Galloway Forest Park, with high hills and rugged scenery. Glen Trool is a tourist attraction but shouldn't fool the walker into believing that he or she need not be fit in order to complete it happily. I was at last beginning to believe I was fit enough.

The Southern Upland Way is marked by lone fence posts with an engraved thistle and directional arrow. We had been following these all the way from Portpatrick. Sometimes they were closely spaced, sometimes not, like today, which is why we got completely lost in a matter of minutes. The area fell absolutely silent as if the forest had stopped to watch how we got out. The owners had put in new roads all over the place, making the map only half useful. Embarrassment is too kind a word.

'Look, guys. We've obviously wandered but if we follow a compass bearing we have *got* to hit the route in the next half mile,' I explained. My confidence was genuine but as anyone who has been in a similar situation knows, cast iron certainties don't always follow. There was, to me, an accommodating nod of heads. Truthfully, I knew how to get out of here, but did the Reivers believe me? And how had this happened so early in the morning?

The area was sopping. Every pole and fern was laced with fat drops
~~~

of water as we struggled north through a comically thick pine jungle where the branches came right down to our knees. I'd never seen such thick growth; it was like walking through non-stop hedges. Then the landscape suddenly opened like a jump cut, and we were in another scene, the promised river, the Water of Trool, fast-flowing but broad and shallow, bubbling over boulders.

This was crossed with ease. It wasn't deep but we were redeemed, weren't we? No one was in the mood for alleluias and *Going to the River* – I was the only Christian anyway. The group stood without exchanging conversation under a thorn tree, the rain lashing down as we removed boots and screwed socks. Two ragged Scottish blackfaces eyed us timidly. Dhal flapped his arms to shoo them away. There was a brief second when the sheep looked nervously at each other, as if expecting the other to decide what to do, before turning and hurrying away like two indignant students in Afghans. Bishwa blew his lips in a rolling raspberry. Where exactly were we?

With the confidence of a sleepwalker I announced from the map the name of one of the riverside cottages alongside: Holm. I was right. We were saved! Alleluia! And don't rivers always feature in the happy-clappy parts of the Bible? Amen to that.

'Oh, bugger this!' I cried in English, introducing the profane. 'Look!' I held up soggy sugar sachets (nicked from the hotel) which were now ruined. The boys hooted with laughter, although to me, personally, it was a little over-done.

The rain increased from a gentle levity to a malicious menace. We hit the road again, a muddy path alongside the river, where wet reeds jabbed our passing calves like cocktail sticks.

The early morning hadn't exactly started brilliantly. I had made a small fool of myself at Newton Stewart's Safeways when paying for some supplies. The girl had taken my Switch card and asked: 'Would you like any cash back?'

Back-footed, it momentarily occurred to me that this was some sort of promotion. She wouldn't be asking if I wanted change, surely?

'Oh, yes please!' I said childishly.

'How much?'

'How much are you giving?'

The lass then took several minutes to explain patiently that this wasn't some give-away. Any sum delivered would be deducted from my card. Had I never heard of cash back? The basic facts of a current account were described in the simplest terms. I caught sight of my oafish face in a mirrored column. The total moron look.

Fortunately, there were only about ten people party to all this, mostly open-mouthed. They probably rushed home to tell the family. I'm sure if I ever return there'll be someone grinning behind a hand while pointing me out with the other.

But that was before we started walking. Now we were getting soaked somewhere to the north. The river, the Water of Trool, took us to a bedrenched Caldons Forestry Commission caravan and campsite whose unfortunate inmates looked utterly woebegone. We, in contrast, were in high spirits and strode through, greeting the campers with unnecessary cheerfulness. They wore that universal Scottish tourist expression: 'We've chosen the wrong sodding week – again.' I don't remember being quite so wet myself, ever. I suspect we came across as altogether too pleased with ourselves.

We entered the glen through marsh which went up to our knees. My thick socks absorbed the wet instantly. It was like marching on sodden sponges. I tried walking them dry but couldn't. My boots just made a series of wheezy wet noises like I was kicking a drowned corpse. The others, though, regularly stopped to wring out their socks. I copied and was amazed at how such a simple measure made such a big difference.

Glen Trool is a five mile gash in the landscape, gouged in the crushing agony of Scotland's glaciation, centred by a deep loch with steep forests on its south side through which a winding path for footsloggers like us was the only thoroughfare. Apparently Robert the Bruce, or maybe his wee brother, had won a battle here. Good luck to him, we thought, trying not to slip on the wet stones which were dangerously strewn with pine needles. One slip would see us tumble down to the loch on our left, but as if stung by the elements, our pace became angrily faster. On this, our third day, the landscape had changed yet again and although the valley sides rose to only 350 metres, their granite cores extruded in long crags, giving a mountainous look.

There was a point when I realised that I had endured two-and-a-half hours back-breaking, muscle-screaming marching and that it was only 10.30 a.m. Just how much exercise can a body take before it affects a man's health adversely instead of improving it? This was a question I had to dwell upon almost every morning while fully aware that this had to continue for another six hours that day and many more days thereafter. I hope those old guys in Nepal are genuinely in need, because, if this situation continued, then so would I.

Stopping at the usual time for coffee I was aghast that no one wanted a break. The coffee breaks were the only moments which I really enjoyed (no hot coffee and cigs could lead to a personal break down) and now even that was being snatched away. Surely I deserve it, and am I not in charge round here? As it happened, apparently not. The rain was heavy and to my colleagues a stop was unthinkable. The Gurkha spirit shone through. We keep walking, pal. You may be the boss but you're not in charge. This is for your own good – no one like us stops in the rain; we keep going. At the moment we're wet and warm; if we stop we'll be wet and cold. They were right, of course, and the march continued. There were forces here beyond my control. For one, we were in the world's only rain forest where the downpour came sideways.

'Are there leeches here?' asked Gyan with beguiling innocence. 'I'm covered in midges,' he added.

'Midges? At this time of day?' I, the local expert, laughed sceptically. Displaying his usual calm, he turned so I could look into his right ear. Sure enough, there was a wee Caledonian midge measuring up for immediate residence. Was I going to say or do anything right today?

For some reason the signposts took us off the route marked on the map and over an irksome summit where we encountered not just waving man-size bracken but a malevolent gale joined the rain. The climb was hard work, made doubly so by being unexpected. It was like being plunged into a giant lettuce salad, a waterfall and Navarone Force 10, made surreal by a bunch of hearty rugby players coming out of nowhere and thundering down the path shouting loudly as we struggled up. We were obliged to stop until they passed – breaking every mountain protocol from the Alps to the Cuillins. I saw Gyan looking upwards, teeth bared, as the last crashed down, hoping to God that none collided with our lot.

Dropping down from the summit to find ourselves on a shale road, with the Galloway Forest now only on our left, I noticed that, at last, I had a phone signal. Despite advertisers claiming that 90% of the population is served by their networks, they are careful not to state 90% of the country. So far, Dumfries & Galloway had proved to be in the frustrating 10% category. I called *The Scotsman* newspaper in Edinburgh with Gyan obligingly holding his dainty ladies' umbrella above me as I hunched over a weeping notebook.

I filed a story about the boys discovering the 'Hello, hen' greeting, and rabbited about Bishwa's blasé assertion that he'd done no real training but had let slip that he'd run 100 kilometres in ten hours just the week before. This was across the South Downs, ending at Brighton. There had been 250 teams of four and his, from the Gurkha Demonstration Company, had not only won but broken the record by an extraordinary sixty-two minutes.

'The guys have been calling me Thulo Neil, Big Neil, but I discovered today that Neil in Gurkhali means Nothing, so in effect I'm the Big Zero!' Gyan and Kali, alert and unashamedly eavesdropping like alert young nephews, gave me the spelling of *thulo*. Dhal had the nerve to announce later he'd completely forgotten that Neil meant Nil, but to be honest, it was more a nickname I'd chosen myself. I had toyed hopefully with Dilbahadur, Brave Heart, but the laughter convinced me to drop the idea.

Let's be honest, their names can confuse. The Gurkhas are recruited mainly from four martial hill tribes: the Rai, the Gurung, the Limbu and the Magar who comprise about 10% of Nepal's population. With such a shortage of surnames the soldiers are nearly always addressed by their forename only, be it by their mother or drill sergeant. Fortunately the shortage of family names has led to a surfeit of forenames. It is not a mark of disrespect to drop Bishwa's clan name. There would be confusion in the ranks if Rifleman Rai was ordered to step forward when there might be two hundred of Rifleman Rais. As if to confuse matters, most, like Gyan, Dhal and Kali, have the middle name Bahadur, meaning Brave.

The shale road sloped downhill with big storm ditches on either side. The hills became wild and rugged, bare of trees, with stony outcrops pro-

Opposite: **Dhal with way marker. Note his thickly-veined legs.**

truding like broken bones revealing how thin was the covering skin. The rain had reduced to a patter. Things must be looking up, I thought far too soon. It became obvious that somehow, when stopping to make my phone call, we had lost Bishwa and Dhal who had gone marching off into the great unknown. Cursing myself, I charged off ahead of Kali and Gyan, shouting. What if they were lost? How much time would it take to find them? Would it affect our timetable?

I bumped into an elderly couple in cagoules. 'Have you seen two Gurkhas?' I yelled into their astonished faces.

'Yes!' they pointed with trembling fingers up the track.

I ran and ran, wondering just how far the boys could have gone in five minutes, becoming slowly certain that they had wandered off route. The rain washed down my face, eyes nearly desalinated, when, still calling out for the missing Reivers, I passed a bothy.

Inside were Dhal and Bishwa, sitting on a damp wooden floor, shirts off, socks and jackets dripping from the rafters, as they quietly went about their lunch. A filthy wooden table took up most of the shed, a single window looked out on to a grey squall-ruffled loch. The hovel looked straight out of a bad day in the mid-West.

'Didn't you hear me calling?'

'Yes,' replied Dhal simply, concentrating on his cuppa, 'Just now.' A fatigue swept through me together with the blissful realisation that we were stopping at last. I'd probably over-reacted. Why hadn't they answered? Suddenly my only concerns were a hot coffee and a cig. Then perhaps a couple of sandwiches. Then a quick coffee, mini Mars bar – and another cig. A life of dissolute pleasure beckoned.

Dhal smoked like a crematorium while Kali loved a Nepalese chewing tobacco not known for its absence of a certain stimulatory content, bordering on the illegal. Kali smoked too, with a pleasure not seen since cigarette advertising became illegal.

Gyan and Kali appeared at the door, making all the usual Gurkha greeting noises with mock solemnity, like they were kids visiting relatives, which were returned with preoccupied giggles as we dug into our lunch.

Our sodden clothes were flung over a beam above but they created their own large raindrops which fell on our huddled shoulders below. To hell with it, we pulled all the stuff down and shoved it into a corner.

'We're doing quite well, eh, Neil?' asked Dhal.

'Well, you are, sitting there with a hot cup of tea!' I smiled. 'Yeah, we're doing fine and it doesn't look like the rest of the day will be difficult walking: mostly downhill forestry roads.' We poked at the map, grunting contentedly. Strangely, I wasn't cold, sitting barefoot in only shorts and polo shirt. The door was open but clouds of steam filled the room coming from our drinks and bodyheat. A notice above my head announced that the bothy was named after a doctor who liked this walk but was now dead.

The comfort of thirty minutes rest is dangerous. Either you become unwilling to move ever again, or your leg muscles seize up and you spend the next ten minutes walking like Douglas Bader. Today though, with the floor so damp, we kept getting to our feet before squatting down again. The lads were anxious to move on too. The prospect of eternal residence in a Galloway bothy faded.

The packs were thrown on again and our hats pulled down, as we headed out into the drizzle. This was the first day Bishwa hadn't brought his video camera, which brought total absorption when he filmed and then silence during the play back. For someone who didn't normally speak much anyway, and given his enthusiasm for the video, this represented a severe limitation to conversation. Kali and Bishwa had arrived at my Edinburgh flat a day earlier than Dhal and Gyan, which allowed them to wander all round the city 'interviewing' passers-by about what they thought of the place. Amazingly they bumped into a couple of my friends who thought it was a set up. I watched the playback with the enchantment of a kid, hardly able to believe the coincidences. Neither Kali nor Bishwa could pronounce my address and at least one taxi driver had to call me on a mobile to interpret their attempts at 'Trinity Crescent.' Kali, himself, could never understand why I wanted to perfect my Gurkhali pronunciation. For instance, the word for please is 'hos'. 'You say it like "hose", Neil, you know, like "hosepipe"'. That's fair enough except that you can say a word with any amount of accents. I wanted the right one, but never quite mastered it. The team had members from all over Nepal, and their pronunciation varied. Apparently, in the days when there were ten Gurkha regiments, each had its own and could be identified. There is no RP Gurkhali, no language to differentiate officer from man, and for two hundred years it has worked perfectly. I needn't have worried.

The route had taken us well to the east, Loch Dee lay on our left with the highest peak we'd yet encountered, the rocky Craiglee at 531 metres, looming behind it. This was the rugged area that had inspired John Buchan's *Thirty-Nine Steps*, and, boy, did it show.

'See these tracks?' I said to Bishwa, pointing to two sets of boot prints leading away from us. 'Everyone has a stronger leg, and when you are tired you favour it. You know how if you were taking a football penalty you'd use your right?' Bishwa nodded, smiling indulgently, as if I was the neighbourhood daft laddie that had to be humoured. 'Well, look at these. Both walkers are putting weight on their right leg. That means they're tired, and at this time of day it can only mean they're carrying large packs.'

We measured the prints alongside our own.

'One's about your height,' said Bishwa, suddenly Tonto.

'In this rain, they can't be far ahead,' I surmised gravely, as if there was deep significance to all this. I was talking crap, of course, but it was based on some sort of intelligent deduction. Now the crap was to have its moment.

As we turned a corner, there they were. A couple, a man and a woman, moving like laden lorries in the motorway slow lane, bearing large packs the size of houses. I let out a laugh. The bullshit had come together beautifully. With our pace, we seemed to trot past them but there was time to say hello. Germans. Having been brought up in Berlin and having spoken the language since before I could read, I rarely miss an opportunity for a gratuitous German joke. To use a motorway image, they were lumbering Dorniers to our throttled forward Hurricanes. I explained we were soldiers from Nepal to looks of utter astonishment.

'Aber was machen Sie hier in Schottland?' (But what are you doing here in Scotland) called the bloke. 'Urlaub!' (holiday) I replied. Their looks transformed into utter confusion. The guys, on the other hand, gave me suspicious glances as if I had been communicating with the enemy. This had happened before and I got the same gravely impassive expression. The question is, what is a Gurkha thinking about when's he's not showing what he's thinking? And should I know about it?

Bishwa and I walked on ahead. Quiet and respectful, Bishwa was organised and intelligent, clearly dedicated to his work and would obviously go far. His pride in being a Gurkha, and one of the best Gurkhas, radiated in a pride which required no words. His slim build and floppy black hair belied a musculature that could have been carved from hardwood. There was not a pinch of fat on him and his legs were great twists of rippling muscle threaded over with veins that pulsed with strength and good health.

I had laughed when we sat in an Edinburgh pub with Bishwa pouring a cup of tea before carefully adding sugar and stirring – and then giving it to Kali, who took it like M' Lord Kali with barely a nod of acknowledgement. 'Ah, yes,' said Gyan, 'but his time will come,' implying that the sunlit uplands of a corporal's high life included all sorts of glamorous perks, including having one's tea poured for one by willing minions.

On the first morning of their stay, I awoke in my flat to crashing and bashing and the sounds of splashing water. In the kitchen I found Kali and Bishwa clad only in shorts, squatting and scrubbing the floor. Enough toast for ten lay piled in a smoking heap. There would have been more but the mysteries of a gas grill had initially defeated the twosome. Kali looked up over a dazzling smile and long cigarette to point delightedly at their work – a floor swirling in suds and water. You had to be there.

And now Bishwa and I were tramping across my homeland, towards a town I'd never heard of in weather I wanted to forget. 'My wife in Nepal is having a baby this week,' he blurted, almost as an aside.

His English, never clear, sometimes let him down but this revelation, stated unambiguously, hit me like a bombshell

'Your wife is having a baby this week?' I repeated, dumbfounded. 'Your first?'

He nodded. 'Dear God, and when are you going to find out? Next week?'

He nodded again, smiling slightly. 'Is this true, Gyan?' I asked aghast. 'Perhaps Bishwa's a dad already and doesn't know it!'

Gyan grinned. 'Someone would phone us,' he announced simply. I was glad to notice that Gyan had stopped adding the English expression 'innit?' to the end of every sentence but the answer was too trite.

'Well,' I countered, 'I think Bishwa ought to be able to phone Nepal a couple of times this week, just to see what's what.'

'Compassionate phone call,' added Gyan quickly, obviously quoting from a well-thumbed welfare guide, and ready to detail it in the accounts. No wonder he's a staff sergeant, I thought.

Bishwa pulled a key ring from his pocket, shyly pointing: 'My wife and me.' In the plastic fob was encased a photo of a dashing couple in dark glasses astride a gleaming motorcycle. They looked very cool.

'Your wife?' I said in genuine surprise. 'She's gorgeous!'

He hummed in pleasure. Gyan then pulled out a photo of his wife, Yashoda, and two boys, Rupen and Rubchen. 'Taken in Bournemouth,' he added casually, as if to say: I've been around, you know. Gyan's wife was a beauty too but the boys were living proof that God is a cartoonist. The two stocky figures at the front were miniature Gyans with the same intelligent look of curiosity (probably evaluating the camera), undeniably and comically their father's sons. The lads were, of course, doing brilliantly at school, top of the class, source of glowing reports and a credit to their parents. I felt a sweep of affection for the whole lot.

'I always wanted to take my wife to Paris,' said Gyan, in a straightforward way, as if telling me the time. What a world, I thought, where a farm boy from Mount Everest could dream of taking his wife to Paris – and now be able to do so.

'I'm building a house in Nepal,' began Gyan.

'A palace!' interrupted Dhal, grinning and catching my eye.

There was a moment's embarrassment. Dhal repeated the word, winking.

'How big is it, Gyan?' I asked.

'Well, I like space,' he began defensively, as if this was vaguely sinful but then gushed proudly: 'Three floors, I think, with high ceilings.'

The 'I think' was less on account of failing memory, more the 'I think' of a pasha deciding. 'I want a fountain in the garden with stones from all over the world, just ordinary stones, so that no one would steal them.' This, one gathered, wasn't off the cuff musing.

'Fountains already!' Dhal, a Buddhist, had to have been Jewish in another life.

The grey wet weather absorbed us again and we fell silent.

Opposite: **The ever-silent Bishwa. Just what is he thinking?**

GURKHA REIVER

Handbooks describe the area's dazzling wildlife but I remember none of it. The road took us to a big Y-shaped loch, Clatteringshaws. Again, a name from my childhood, one I had always imagined was spelled Clatteringshores and was one of those charming names taken from the literal of waves clattering upon the shores. Perhaps it is. The rain had stopped but a cold wind blew across its rippling brown expanse. A diversion took us along a white-taped corridor across the rocks on the loch's edge. Large lorries were being loaded with long wet logs, their barks bruised and scuffed with pale wood scratches shining like exposed sores. The wind whipped bitter round our bare legs.

The Way continued down through moorland with a plantation on our left, Forrest Estate, owned by Fred Olsen, surprisingly, but we were cruising. The miles were being eaten up, not quite at the gallop but with a remorseless amble that never slowed. In the west stood another record peak, the 746 metre Meikle Millyea, but the Galloway hills were behind us now and we were headed down the Garroch Glen to our evening destination. Somehow, I had done that stupid of things, pull my jacket drawstring so that one end was now in the middle of my back. For two miles I fiddled and picked to get it back but then, in a wee tantrum, pulled the whole blasted thing out.

Funny thing about maps and walking: there's a tendency to say 'Only five miles and we're home.' Kali had glanced at the map and delivered the saw (one I'd never heard before): 'Always add an extra mile.' But we weren't listening. We were crossing the map like ants on a mission. Not long now!

At about four o'clock we passed our couple from England. The man gave us a tight smile but looked tired. 'My wife was determined to beat you today!' he grinned sadly.

The valley was now full of alder and birch, and Bishwa and I were way ahead, walking like we were on stimulants, when the route suddenly transformed into a series of short steep climbs over bracken which we tackled with an angry aggression. Then, at last, was the long slope into St John's Town of Dalry (a name I have never seen shortened) with us bounding down, across a main road and through some buildings to a large soft field whose far border marked our day's end.

Campbell met us by the footbridge that crossed the Water of Ken, part of a complicated river system that enters the Solway Firth near Kirkcudbright. The attractive church beside it holds the bodies of yet more Covenanters. Eventually Gyan and Kali traipsed in, grinning. But where was Dhal?

Gyan, Campbell and I jumped into the van. I was sure he'd not seen one of the last signposts and had continued on the main road. To reach where we supposed him to be was not a short drive and again I felt that anxiety that can't be shared. Sure enough, we found our lone Reiver happily trudging southwards off to England along the A762. I felt like the commander of an aircraft carrier when a missing flight at last arrives safely. Dhal wasn't remotely bothered, of course.

Campbell and I shared a room in a nearby farmhouse, while our salesman and banker Keith stayed in one of those old sandstone country hotels in need of several million pounds' worth of renovation. The others were in a modern B&B only yards away. The village was tiny but it also boasted another hotel, the Clachan Inn, a classic low-beamed, stonewalled country pub with 'rooms'. The owner had written to me offering rooms for nothing only days before, having read about us in the papers. Unfortunately, by then I couldn't switch bookings but reserved suppers. We couldn't expect free meals though.

When I booked the accommodation in this village, there had been unpleasantness. Deposits are normally required but these were demanded – along with being informed that our hosts were not keen on walkers who use up the precious hot water. I couldn't understand this at the time. Why would a lonely village B&B on the Southern Upland Way discourage walkers? The warning signs were all there.

When our four Nepalese arrived the elderly landlady suddenly and aggressively wanted to know whether they wanted supper or not. It was an unexpected display of rudeness, not to mention alarming exhibition of spittle-roped false teeth. I remembered in a flash how rude this individual had been on the phone. In fact, she had been difficult to get on the phone at all. If she had wanted to tell me about suppers, there had been plenty of opportunity.

'Er. No. The Clachan is giving us supper for free!' This information, as you can imagine, was received with all the calmness of Basil Fawlty losing his winnings to a German. The Scottish Tourist Board, I fancied, were already drafting a restraining order.

'Did you see that lady?' asked Gyan later, part mystified, part indignant, as if describing a petty crime that defied belief. The welcome at the Clachan was as different as to suggest the proprietors were of another breed, culture and possibly species. Its brochure went a bit too far, though, announcing 'The Inn's sporting heritage is attractively revealed in the fine range of *objets art'* – and a wonderful atmosphere too – if shaky French. But the Clachan was a busy pub full of pleasant people eating excellent food in numbers not seen anywhere on a Monday night in the surrounding hundred miles. The staff welcomed us with big smiles from behind the bar, with the greeting: 'We're ready when you're ready'. (Nowadays the Clachan has computerised information in the bar describing the Southern Upland Way.)

The team sat at a long single table and wolfed down the stuffed mushrooms, the steak and chips, the turf 'n' surf and the hearty sweets with the hunger of true reivers. We even ordered sandwiches for the morning to discover there were 'special fillings' like lamb and chutney or coronation chicken, plus free crisps and club biscuits.

'What's the best thing for blisters?' I asked.

To my surprise this brought about a bitter argument with Dhal stating bluntly that to burst one would lead to infection while Kali was appalled, claiming that combat soldiers had no option but to burst blisters and careful use of antiseptic would avoid infection. While Dhal's voice remained steadfastly deep, Kali's rose to near hysterics. What should have been a dinner table conversation had descended into a fractious brawl.

'Gyan, can you settle this?' I asked helplessly. He looked away, impassive. The message was that this would blow over and he was keeping out of it anyway. British officers have long relied on senior NCOs to interpret the men's actions (and not just in the Gurkhas); this was as good a time as any to observe the practice. Gyan was right. In a minute the 'blistering' row was forgotten. It was to return though, and Kali was later to over-react to one of my decisions, but after this evening I knew not to depress myself about it. For myself, punctured blisters are defi-

Opposite: **St John's Town of Dalry: the bridge that saw us home.**

nitely liable to infect.

The support team, Keith and Campbell, had spent the day selling to the wise burghers of Dumfries and were as hungry as we were. Our third day, seventy-something miles gone, and Keith had not yet greeted the team upon arrival. Kali wanted to know why and was unmoved to hear that Keith had been taking a bath when we arrived. Dhal thought this was a joke, given our respective needs for a bath, and Gyan had to shush him. For the record, Keith was tired, cold, and had been on his feet all day and certainly wasn't needed to greet the lads coming in. All the same, Dhal and Kali were puzzled. Bishwa, of course, said nothing.

Post supper, who should we meet, sitting slumped as if in dumb shock, but our English couple, he of the aggressive demeanour and she of the magnificent bust. They were silent, staring ahead, and didn't appear to recognize me. 'Hi, we're the Gurkhas who keep seeing you!' I said with Gyan by my side.

The man's eyes flashed in slow recognition. Our appearance differed from the daytime uniform of shorts and red shirts but how could he fail to know us? His eyes betrayed utter fatigue and it dawned on me that I hadn't seen anyone so jaded in ages, perhaps since those two English guys yesterday.

'You know what we've been trying to do, don't you? My wife and I read about you in the papers and we decided we'd try and beat you. No luck, even though we've been getting up earlier and earlier in the morning. Now, we're too tired to go on and have decided to go home tomorrow.'

We were amused but utterly baffled as to why anyone in their right minds would have attempted such a thing. We hadn't proved anything about our superiority. They had large packs, for God's sake, while we bore only our lightweight *jholas*, a rucksack halfway between a small and large pack. They were not young either and should have realised long ago that their o'er vaulting ambition would only bring grief.

For myself, I discovered two things: a hot shower now stung my legs and a blister the size of a half ping pong ball on the inside of my right heel thankfully didn't hurt but, strangely, tickled.

The rain had fallen nearly all day: now the night was falling. We were a team of several members, but a team, a single team.

IV

St John's Town of Dalry to Sanquhar

~~~

Despite the implications of many facetious text message questions from friends, my feet were not sore but my legs needed time to get going in the morning. It had taken three days to realise the folly of brand new woollen socks every morning. After the first half an hour the fibre settled, requiring the laces to be tightened. An old hillwalking pro later told me that for maximum comfort you should wear the same socks for several days. There's an upper limit involved here, obviously, and after the soaking of yesterday, I think I'd have worn new ones today anyhow.

Our walk would be forty kilometres or twenty-five miles, hitting exactly the necessary daily average. The previous three days had each been slightly below target but the route to Sanquhar was through different country yet again, one of big hills with grown-up contours, over rough moorland. These were the true uplands of the Upland Way where the route becomes higher and tougher. The guidebook and website thundered that 'only the *extremely* fit and experienced walker should attempt this stretch in a day' but the guys were undaunted. In fact, one wondered if 'daunt' had a Nepali equivalent. By now this was a way of life, where our focus was only on reaching destinations safely and as quickly as possible without hurting ourselves.

I didn't start the day brilliantly by accidentally calling Gyan 'my girl' instead of 'my lad' – easily done in Gurkhali. *Keta* is a boy but *Keti* is a girl. It should be obvious, shouldn't it? After all, the word Gurkha is

Overleaf. ***Left:*** **The Earlstoun Burn. All footbridges are in excellent condition.** ***Right:*** **The first moorland east of St John's Town of Dalry. We could have had the Battle of the Little Big Horn here. The distant animals are not buffalo but black Galloways.**
~~~

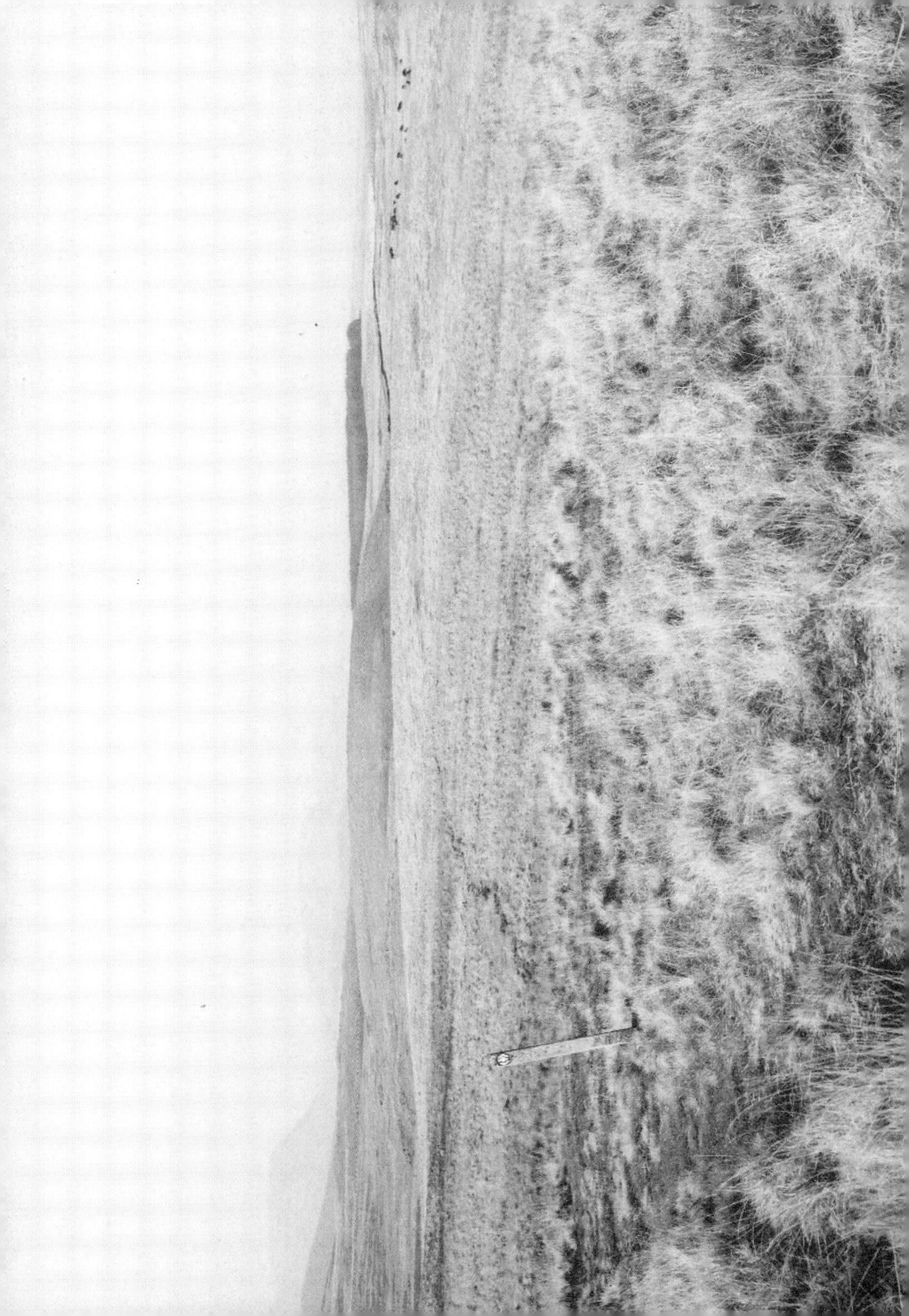

clearly male. But for Latin scholars like me an 'a' ending is unthinkingly female.

It was a beautiful morning that saw us stepping directly out from the B&B and on to the Way, sun in our eyes, up through the village before plodding through the type of fields ideal for dairy herds, thick luscious and green, and still damp from the day before. It was wonderfully reassuring to discover that this little village, with its beautiful cottages, also has an old-fashioned Bank of Scotland based in what could have been a former manse: a stone-built house with high ceilings and large front windows. Is it doubly reassuring to realise it has no ATM? I think so. The police station is rarely manned but does have a 'hot line' telephone to the cerebral crimebusters in downtown Dumfries. All you have to do is lift the handset and inform the ever-vigilant polis down the line about the dastardly deeds carried out in St John's and doubtless they'll come hurrying in a Ford Prefect with blue light flashing. This dazzling prospect, not surprisingly, rarely arises.

Dhal had picked up a walking stick from somewhere, and with a sudden roar, charged up a steep slope, whirling it round like a propeller, shouting and laughing loudly. Obviously, this was the equivalent of gunning the engine. For a second I winced at the pain this would bring before giving a loud yell and galloped up the slope myself, feeling the blood suddenly flow and my spirits soar. My engine fired with a roar of happiness. The gang behind was instantly on my heels, hollering and howling, metaphorically waving kukris above them like a re-enactment of the Heights of Dargai. Had we run into anyone, I suspect they'd have been mown down in one of the least likely accidents ever seen in Dumfriesshire.

The author E. D. 'Birdie' Smith, who commanded a Gurkha company in Italy during the war, once recalled a night when the men had to attack an unreconnoitered village. Having taken many casualties in the days before, the men showed little enthusiasm when asked to take on unnumbered Germans in the dark. Birdie had goaded them with their motto 'It is better to die a hero than live a coward,' until the valley echoed with the war cry 'Ayo Gurkhali'– the Gurkhas are coming. Then, with a blood-freezing crescendo, they rose from their slit trenches and ran screaming into the darkness at an unknown enemy. Birdie reckons he lost total control of at least one platoon, a third of his men, as they charged into the blackness. The job was eventually done, but no one present on either side could ever forget the unholy intensity that resounded through the air that night, chilling every soldier for miles. There was something primeval, touching a folk fear memory, disturbing but elating. One thing was sure, the Gurkhas fought like Berserkers and would do so again – but not this morning.

The landscape opened up with low hills to the north west, Knockwhirn, Benniner and Moorbrock Hill, like lines of turtles behind an open moorland, prairie-like with brilliant dry grass rippling to distant horizons under huge blue skies. The hills are merely rows of petrified sand-dunes, covered with a thin skin of grass and earth which explains the panorama's softness. Distant dark green patches denoted entire forestry plantations but the over-riding colours were pale and faded beneath a glorious summer sky. Songbirds twittered and piped, performing flirty aerobatics while others, chests out, clung sentinel to lone dry thistles, singing out a declaration of territory – or was it just through sheer joy? It was irritating that I couldn't identify most of what appeared to be a flypast of half of the *The British Book of Birds*, Moorland Section. A male winchat tic-tic-ticked sharply, a bird that took a long time to spot despite its red-brown breast. We saw no harriers or hobbies, not even a buzzard, and more surprisingly, never heard the liquid unwinding call of the curlew. We were too late in the year to witness that heathland joy, the skylark, Shelley's blithe spirit. The five minute warble when the bird, uniquely, ascends vertically in a hover like a micro-helicopter until nearly out of sight and then descends singing continuously, is one of the most heart-lifting sounds in the human experience. But their calls cease in mid-July. Our hearts beat in rapture nonetheless. This nameless forgotten area was not for working – but poetry and art – not labour.

There were butterflies unknown to me. Small wings were fluttering everywhere. Most were red admirals and painted ladies who both, astonishingly, migrate from North Africa – a fact learned as a suspicious boy and never quite accepted as entirely true. But apart from some ragged tups

Overleaf. ***Left:*** **Bishwa climbs one of the many excellent fence crossing points.** ***Right:*** **Kali eyes up my camera, secure in the knowledge that it is not the one he lost on a train.**

GURKHA

nestling in the sunshine, the landscape was empty. How could we be so remote without being in the Highlands? And how did Wyoming get to be in Dumfries and Galloway? They could have had the Battle of the Little Big Horn here. It was Scottish scenery unknown to me, empty of roads and empty of practically everything bar rolling hills, white with grass under a blue vastness.

It was sheer happiness that prompted Kali to begin singing: gentle folk songs generally involved a lonely hill boy and a beautiful girl. His soft mellifluous voice perfectly appropriate, he sang more or less continually for the next few days, earning the nickname Radio Kali. Julie Andrews, thankfully, was not part of the repertoire. In fact, I was beginning to feel slightly high. Perhaps breakfast had included an elixir or a touch of some euphoric drug, though given our landlady's absence of good cheer, I doubt it somehow: the woman who put hospital in hospitality! Right now, I imagine the tourist board inventing a special minus category to fit her unique status.

Our pace was continuous though, never in big strides but quick and brisk, almost a trot. Roads had slipped away below the horizon and the team found itself in an uncultivated wilderness which perhaps explained why it seemed to be one immense butterfly farm; no farmer would ever have used herbicide here. I hadn't spent two consecutive days hillwalking for years, and now I was on my fourth. We crossed the Earlstoun Burn.

'If this was Nepal, Neil, a family would come and set up a farm here,' said Gyan wistfully, to ready agreement from the others.

'Yes, they would just take it,' added Dhal.

'Could anyone here do that, Neil? asked Kali.

'Er, no. These hills may look empty but they belong to someone, believe you me.'

'But who would find out? This area is not being used by anyone.'

'I know, Kali,' I replied, 'but the soil here is too poor for crops. The rain is too wet. The drainage is bad and wind would blow away the top soil.'

'I would steal this land,' confided Kali, unbowed. In his homeland the earth was even poorer, where potatoes grew to only the size of ping-pong balls, and irrigation and drainage were achieved by terraces built over a thousand years. Gyan's father owned some pastures in the lowlands, but at 5,000 feet, that's higher than Ben Nevis. Yes, everything's relative.

Dry and firm underfoot, we were making good progress and mid-morning I was able to announce that we had just walked off the edge of the second of eight maps. By the end of the day we would have hit the ninety-mile figure and be nearly half way to the North Sea. If the sun kept up I might get a good tan too.

The previous three days had improved my fitness, and steady climbing up the whale-back hills was now no great difficulty although it was a surprise to discover how much cooler one felt having removed, to me, an unaccustomed hat. We passed another couple on an upward slope, our knees lifting casually and breath coming in healthy deep lungfuls. These two were Dutch. 'From the lowest country in the world, meet some people from the highest country in the world!' I laughed. They nodded and waved us on completely nonplussed. Perhaps they didn't understand: either that or I was more out of breath than I thought.

As we approached the 580 metre summit of Benbrack, the air filled with engine noise, the unmistakable scouring sound of an RAF fighter edging the horizon. We stopped and looked north where a dark shape peeled and came towards us like a smoky arrow. The aircraft flashed across the route fifty metres ahead of us with a great boom, nearly grazing the rounded summit, while we waved and cheered like crazy.

We'd been close enough to see the pilot's face, we told each other. I'm sure he'd have seen us, don't you? Oh, yes, couldn't have missed us, five blokes in red waving away. We were nearly part of an RAF exercise: search and destroy the Gurkha Reivers. They'll be on this route at such and such a time and then POW! Perfect training if you think about it. Yeah, except we never told the RAF. I'm sure though, that they'd have been interested in the idea, yes? Neil, next time you *will* remember?

Minutes later, from the same direction, came three bi-planes in a wobbling formation, their flight uncannily slow and practically inaudible. I've never seen a formation of bi-planes anywhere before and for them to be droning along in the wake of an RAF Jaguar was a surreal coincidence. It was as if we were witnessing the past through some Scottish time window. We never did get to the bottom of this spectre.

Our meal breaks had been trimmed into refreshment stops, but there was still time to phone *The Scotsman* diarist, Simon Pia, and report on the latest developments at the front. I could only describe how I'd warned the lads that we were coming up to a big hill, something like 300 metres, before remembering that Dhal was from Annapurna and the others from Everest. Simon was able to tell me that his office had already received £50 worth of donations. In addition, the staff had contributed a further £60. The Ministry of Defence had been on too, reminding them that the Gurkha Welfare Trust provided pensions only for those 11,500 surviving wartime Gurkhas who had served 'for the duration' and not the 25,000 other retired Gurkhas who had served the necessary fifteen years and receive a MoD pension, recently doubled.

'At least somebody's reading all this,' I laughed. Simon's deep voice grumbled in grudging humour, threatening to describe how I'd been getting piggy backs up and down dale.

'Why do you think I chose four Gurkhas if it wasn't the ideal number for stretcher bearing?' I replied. Later I was to learn that the eventual eight reports that appeared in *The Scotsman* generated the biggest response of any other story that year – bar a hysterical series concerning Fanny Craddock prompted by the famous faux pas: 'I hope all your doughnuts taste like Fanny's.'

There was an opportunity too to call my assistant, Leigh, back in Edinburgh, before the signal disappeared. I had only bought this, my first mobile phone, the week before – an important day in a man's life you know – and was still at that Jesus-aren't-these-things-wonderful stage. I was also at the Jesus-I'm-not-using-this-thing-too-often stage. Things back at work were tootling along, with money pouring in. I had risked one display ad in the *Scotsman* and the cash washed in like a river. We'd repeated the tactic in the *Herald*, the *Mail* and the *Express* and even more had winged its way. Only Aberdeen's *Press & Journal* gave us the space for nothing. I had written to every letters' page in the Scottish press, dailies and weeklies, signing myself, for extra effect, with Gyan's name. We even started getting mail addressed only to 'Staff Sergeant Gyanbahadur Tamang, Gurkha Welfare Trust, Edinburgh'.

While this was proof positive of the nation's generosity, it also confirmed a level of naïvety; many envelopes contained actual folding cash! We had over £20,000 before leaving Edinburgh and now the total was past

£25,000. Our expenses had already been paid – this was all clear profit. My initial target had been £10,000, big enough to be respectable but small enough to exceed. There never is a charity fundraiser that doesn't find morale boosted by breaking its target, but as the target figure is entirely arbitrary, care must be taken choosing it. I've seen some projects regard themselves as failures solely because they missed an over-optimistic start figure. The target is an artifice anyway, entirely up to you, so get it right.

I stubbed out the phone like I'd been doing it all my life. All of us had mobiles, I noticed, and yet two years before they were but expensive, complicated aspirations. Kali's love of expensive gadgets extended to cameras. 'I once lost £1,000's worth on a train,' he told me with quiet pride.

It was impossible not to smile with Kali around. His boyish grin always prompted a return, and his bewilderingly innocent take on the world was always worth a laugh. 'I have been reading about when England was a colony of France,' he began with great seriousness before it dawned on me he was talking about the Norman Conquest. 'What is this Hotel Mike Victor?' he'd inquired as we walked down an Edinburgh street. How long would it have taken you to work out he was talking about HMV? Nearly forty, he had had his contract extended several times as the British Army began to grasp the foolishness of retiring first-class Gurkhas after only fifteen years.

Owning a specialist tea plantation near Darjeeling, over the border in India, he was clearly a man that worried about the big things in life albeit with his own unique perspective. Fascination as to my single marital status bubbled over one evening when, with hands brought together like he was wrestling with one of the enigmas of our time, he pronounced: 'Is big mystery, no?' Similarly, Leigh at twenty-four and not yet married, was, like me, earnestly assured that Nepalese partners could be available. Just say the word. Noticing that Leigh didn't finish her supper, our man gave the gallant reassurance: 'Leigh, you don't have to fast!' Flattery was part of his makeup, and perhaps culture too, so that when I asked if he'd be glad to go back to Nepal, his response was an enthusiastic affirmative until

Overleaf. ***Left:*** **Dhal, cool as ever, and on the lookout to bag mice, adders and passing game birds.** ***Right:*** **That special regard. Gyan on PR duty with Dhal piping up in the background.**

he stopped and with a magnificent attempt at sincerity, added: 'Of course, I will be sad to miss you.'

Concern for his fellow man was his watchword. It was, of course, Kali that gave me details of a forgotten widow who was too weak to register at one of Nepal's twenty-four Gurkha Welfare Centres. Invited for supper with my parents, he arrived bearing a huge pot plant which flourishes yet, known only as the Gurkha plant. Allergic to alcohol, he made do on tea or orange juice, but as a Buddhist-animist, he was also the world's only meat-eating vegetarian as 'it would insult the gods not to eat their offerings.' There was another contradiction about Kali: why was he, in uniform, smart as a carrot but in mufti the only Gurkha in Britain to wear a shirt he'd clearly not ironed, with one collar leaping free and a tie that didn't lie straight? Out of uniform, Kali was Nepal's answer to William Brown. His English aside, he was a superb communicator with a clumsy inability to shake hands which was always both charming and genuine.

Kali won people over in seconds; there was no bad in him. Slight of build, he was also immensely strong in a way that spoke volumes as to his hardy childhood. Kali was a man to have with you whatever the situation. I also suspect that, despite the boy-man smile, he had that country boy lack of sentimentality about killing if it was the right course of action. He provided many memorable moments on Gurkha Reiver and I wouldn't have swapped him for a million pounds' worth of sponsorship.

At some point I realised that young Bishwa had disappeared over the horizon, probably to Glasgow, and without a map, could have got lost. We could not stop for a coffee until we found him. Would my memory of him in blue shorts and sockless plimsoles be my last? His phone was blandly off, not a surprise but incandescently annoying. The path took us down through more knee-high white grass before we spotted his red shirt resting on the valley below us, between Cairn Hill and Black Hill. Only when we drew close did we realise he was dozing, laid out as if for a pyre on a neat pile of cross-laid logs, a Hindu funeral *ghat*. He yawned like a dog before rejoining us, fresh-legged as a colt. A reprimand would have been stupid. Those logs though looked very comfortable.

The Way sadly took us away from the prairie-like grasslands and again we found ourselves in cool anonymous forest. While nearly every hill has a name in these parts, the forestry men rarely get round to giving names to their plantations. This one, for those with a map, is located between the quaintly titled Fortypenny Hill and Polskeoch Rig.

Dhal stooped beside the roots of a pine, clearly stalking something. We stopped to watch. What had he seen this time? There was a slap as his right hand hit the forest floor and a hoot of delight. 'Got you, little man!' he grinned. His left hand was holding a field mouse with whiskers twitching in surprise beneath big bewildered black eyes, as if the danger he was in hadn't yet dawned and was still in the 'Oh shit!' stage. Not a look of panic, more sheepish regret, the one you wear when you back the car into a bollard but not the one when the vehicle is driving at 100 mph towards a wall. Sort of 'oh-no-look-at this-will-you?' But Dhal had no intention of harming him, and placed the wee rodent back beside the pine. It surprised no one that it disappeared with the laggardly speed normally associated with an absent-minded professor strolling across the quad. He never knew how lucky he was. The only mouse caught in Scotland that day by a Buddhist.

'How on earth did you catch him?' I asked.

'You put one hand in front of his face and then bring down other hand with a big bang behind him. The mouse then flies into the hand in front of him. He can't help it. His brain sees it as somewhere safe.' I have never heard of such a thing but can testify that it works, and works brilliantly. But how did Dhal spot said beastie in the first place? That's the first skill, as I'd seen with the hen pheasant, and comes from within.

Keen to show I wasn't a total ignoramus, I asked aloud: 'Did you know that the lodge-pole pine is so-named because the North American Indians used it for their teepees and Sitka is a place in Alaska?' Of course, Dhal knew both these facts. He'd read the same guidebook as me the night before.

Upon eventual exit from the forest's gloom, there was a long valley to negotiate with substantial brooding hills on either side. We marched four kilometres down the surfaced road with the Scaur Water on our right. This waterway held other associations, those of actress Joanna Lumley, who lived here. I had written to many famous people a letter of 'blackmail', explaining that the word came from the Borders and would they kindly be blackmailed into giving a small sum. About a quarter of our MPs and MSPs replied enclosing cheques, some announcing that they had too many claims upon their salaries but they'd make an exception for this one. Mike Russell of the SNP phoned me up saying how his father had been in the diplomatic corps and had always felt that the Gurkhas had been given a raw deal.

There was a strong response from SNP politicians although the single largest donation came from Charles Kennedy. We collared a lot of celebs too, including Jimmy Logan and George MacDonald Fraser. The latter's book, *The Steel Bonnets,* is the definitive work on the Border reivers and needed no explanation as to the word's origin. The House of Lords was a happy hunting ground for us too. Robert McNeil, *The Scotman*'s witty (is *witty* enough for you, Rab?) columnist replied to our blackmail letter confessing a long affair with an actress and alluded to perversions with a python as well. But foremost was the support from a real actress, Joanna Lumley. I had worked with her before but was thrilled with her immediate cheque plus a Gift Aid Certificate meaning we could claim another 28% from the Inland Revenue. Of our eventual three thousand donors, she was the only one savvy enough to have done this unasked. Major James Lumley was a famous Gurkha officer, Chindit and all round cool guy. Daughter Joanna had been born in Kashmir just after the war, but with Indian independence had moved with 6th Gurkha Rifles to Kuala Lumpur in Malaya. She was to write several letters of encouragement to Gurkha Reiver and her mum raised funds in a book sale too.

My thoughts turned towards La Lumley this afternoon because I knew we were passing her country cottage, out here in this sun-dappled valley where the words 'isolation' and 'total' went together like Eddie and Patsy. Joanna had written of her understandable frustration at not being able to see us: 'Alas, I can't wriggle free even for a photograph – it's a great blow as you're walking practically over our cottage's doorstep. I'm completely tied up filming on location from now until Christmas and don't even get weekends. I'm so full of admiration – you'll be going at a hell of a lick.' The girl couldn't help herself, I reasoned, and who can blame her? It was a letter that saw the light of day whenever whoever I was speaking to stopped to draw breath.

The valley was sheltered by looming rounded mountains with intimidating names like 'Cloud Hill' which, for a depressing moment, I thought we'd have to climb.

'Look, Neil, horse! We're not far from village!' exclaimed Kali in total defiance of the map.

Sure enough, a white horse grazed on the slopes above us. I looked enquiringly.

'In Nepal horses are only kept on the edges of villages,' explained Gyan, sotto voce.

One stop was always made bang on 4 p.m. as Kali hunkered down to listen to the World Service's Nepali broadcast. This nearly always entailed a plane crash which brought yelps of anguish. Nepal has a horrendous flight safety record but Gyan lightened the mood by announcing that the Royal Nepal Airlines Corporation was known as 'Really Not Altogether Certain'.

The road turned south following the stream, writhing snake-like between the valley's interlocking shoulders to flow past Ms Lumley's door only two miles away but Bishwa and I headed upwards in another direction, north east along a path leading to a notch between two peaks.

'Better wait here until they catch up,' I breathed, slightly concerned as to why Gyan, Kali and Dhal were suddenly on a go-slow. My pocket binoculars picked them up easily, ambling down the road like three oblivious gentlemen on a Sunday afternoon stroll with walking sticks 'n' all.

Anxious and annoyed, I wondered what had happened in the last thirty minutes. Bishwa's sleepy look of contentment gave me no clue. We moved further up the pass but not so that we lost sight of them, then waited again. A splendid shepherd, Charles Weir, and his collie who had come to walk us into the village below appeared on the skyline. This guy was one of the most decent men you'd ever meet. A native of Sanquhar, he'd worked most of his life as a fireman in Manchester only to return to his beloved hills and train sheepdogs. He was the sort of man you blessed unaware. He knew all about us and spoke of a huge welcome in Sanquhar, about three miles away. I cast my eye down at our rambling threesome, wondering what was going on and how long it would take us to cover the three miles.

Eventually they caught up and we tramped down the hill, with the Lowthers and their golf-ball radar dominating the eastern skyline. Bishwa's uninhibited approach to sheep shit brought smiles when he repeatedly threw the stuff around the hill for the dog to chase, disregarding the finer points of hygiene. I made a mental note to avoid any offers of Bishwa's apples.

We stepped off the moorland and on to the village's approach road. Still Gyan and Co went at a mystifyingly slow pace. I called 'Cheeto!' (Hurry!) but received only a clenched teeth smile. We entered the town from the west, then had to walk right to the other end through the grounds of the old Crichton stronghold, Sanquhar Castle, to meet our reception committee who were immense in number and fairly jumping with joy. I couldn't believe either the numbers or their genuine pleasure at meeting us. There were about a hundred people in the first group, old soldiers in their blazers and regimental headgear – mostly Royal Marines' green berets – and a whole bevy of British Legion office bearers.

It was here as we gathered to speechify that I finally understood what had been going on when I overheard one guy ask Gyan. 'So you've got an ulcer?' The reply: 'Well, I'll have to see when I take my boots off.'

Gyan had blisters and the others had slowed down, covering for him, not wishing to show up their staff sergeant and friend! God! Why hadn't I seen this? I'd actually appointed Gyan as i/c feet! What kind of leader was I?

The ellipse of Sanquhar's citizenry suddenly doubled. I knew what to do. My speech was inspired: we were on the path to glory, a path that had now stopped at the fabled Sanquhar, home to heroes and an all round wonderful place. There were laughs and cackles, but they approved mightily and a welcoming warmth was released in waves.

Gyan followed up with a cracking left to my right. The surviving Gurkhas in Nepal, he said, would hear all about the wonder that is Sanquhar. To massive cheers we were led off by the town's piper.

'Hey!' grinned Dhal: 'We're famous!'

Our party crossed the main street, slightly bemused, to discover that behind crush barriers, cheering and clapping, was the town's entire population. The triumphal march was unfortunately curtailed after only twenty metres by our arrival at the lads' B&B, leaving the townsfolk further up the road, who were expecting some sort of pageant, bewildered.

Alone but adored in the middle of the High Street (the dangerous A76 which dominates the place) I found myself waving like Robbie Williams, when Campbell's van drove up. Someone gave me a £10 note and I was quick to give the gold-plated crossed-kukri lapel badge in return, but the rest was a blur. I hopped into the vehicle, pop star-like, acknowledging the masses who stretched for the half mile to my own B&B, waving happily. The excited *Upper Nithsdale News*, the *soi disant* 'Wee Paper', later described (front page, this) how the police had prevented a full-blown march up the street, before adding that the Reivers were accompanied by Neil Griffiths MP, Edinburgh South. Obviously, one of us wasn't famous enough.

My B&B was top quality, where the landlady's welcome was so warm it bordered on sexual invitation. An attractive blonde of my own age, it would have been an invitation I'd have been happy to accept except she was married. I was sharing the room with Campbell and the only stiff thing about me was my knees.

Sanquhar is Campbell's home town, a fiercely Protestant community, which led to him asking, with a wide-eyed intensity, if he could borrow my blue Gurkha tie instead of the normal green one. Religious observation, meaning mostly religious intolerance, is taken very seriously in small-town Scotland. Campbell couldn't be seen in public here in anything as rabidly pro-Rome as a green tie. People would talk, avoid him in the street, and his own mother might disown him. In short, wearing green could be his ruination.

Relaxed, I sat later on the patio, having bathed and changed into a suit, though blissfully barefoot against the flagstones, debating as to whether I was just lucky or just very lucky. God, I felt fit. Sore, yes but exhausted, no. Our hostess laid on an enormous supper – this was about 6.30 p.m. Most of Scotland has what is called 'tea' at around 6 p.m. I attacked it like a wolf while the blonde made jokes about how much water I drank, using some unfunny comment about the Southern Way Mooth – which I took to be her pronunciation of 'mouth'. I just wanted to be worshipped, receiving only hosannas and uncritical adulation: none of this jocose chumminess, thank you. Her over-familiarity was, of course, an affront to my august dignity. I frowned over the fork, deciding that I was too tired to argue, but if she were available in my room at, shall we say midnight, all would be forgiven.

The British Legion had laid on a party upstairs in a pub called the Crown Inn on the main street where Keith's stall was going great guns.

This was no mean feat as he'd been working the town all day in the car park opposite. Once again, straight donations had been the order of the day. The room was low ceilinged and hot with a happy cross of age groups, from wee girls to grey old men. The photos show me healthily rosey, surrounded by country folk from central casting.

It's never easy to give a speech but I was up for it and knew by now what the audience wanted. I could feel the wish for praise and sense the gratification when it hit home.

Gyan began with the tremendous: 'Today's visit is not just heroic but historic; the first visit by Gurkhas to Sanquhar.' His eyes so wide with sincerity, I nearly giggled. He was, however, interrupted by a glassy-eyed pensioner who reckoned that a retired Gurkha officer had passed through in the 1960s. Backfooted, poor old Gyan struggled to regain the moment. He did, of course, but no thanks to our boy, star of *Total Recall*. The tightly packed audience made no attempt to shush the old git (in fact some had loudly and seriously concurred: 'Aye, Jim's right') and Gyan was obliged to patiently absorb the contradiction before continuing like a pro. *Shyabash!*

The town had done everything a visiting group could want. The Post Office, Britain's oldest, had been collecting for months and we were presented with, not just several cheques, but an embroidered Legion pennant. Three Legion branches between them gave £1,083 while a number of local businesses made contributions too.

Gyan accepted all the plaudits and donations like a minor royal and then produced two gifts that Leigh and I had put together. One was a teddy bear in Gurkha uniform that brought oohs and aahs, while the other was a Certificate of Appreciation to the good folk of Sanquhar, signed by the team. These went down a bomb, especially when Gyan expressed the hope, as if he were Max Bygraves or something, that everyone would remember this evening whenever their eyes fell on either. It was as a shameless exhibition of heartstring pulling as you ever saw.

The evening confirmed what I'd always known about the Royal British Legion Scotland. To some it's a mysterious yet benevolent organ-

Opposite: **Our treasurer, Keith Halley (left) with his hands on the money.**

isation, full of ex-military types with their own shibboleths and stories. They're a bunch whose principles seem dated, but in fact are timeless – good fellowship and service to others. These tonight were good folk and I found them humble and uplifting.

It didn't take long for someone to ask quietly which foot we kicked with, in that earnest disingenuous Scottish way, the unbelievable caveat that your answer doesn't matter at all really – but I've simply got to know. That the visitors were Protestant (me), Buddhist (Dhal and Gyan), Hindu (Bishwa whom I had earlier been led to believe was a Buddhist) and animist (Kali, of course) was good news and, apparently, not often encountered hereabouts. No matter that we weren't all Proddies; no one was You Know What, and that was the main thing. The revelation was brought to happy conclusion by the declaration that Dhal was a Rangers man. Ibrox has, of course, for too long suffered an unbecoming dearth of Buddhists. The Legionnaires relaxed. Our shared culture was confirmed yet again when Gyan, outlining how remote was his home village, explained that the nearest bus stop was three days' walk away. 'Aye,' added a local, removing pipe from mouth: 'That sounds just like our bus service.'

Bishwa was unusually silent that night. Campbell approached me sideways, sidled, to whisper that Bishwa had left his black lace-up shoes in St John's Town of Dalry. I blinked in incredulity that this paragon could do anything thoughtless at all, and then, like a father, took in his immaculate regimental mufti with a new eye: the ensemble was lifted by two hulking hiking boots. 'Just get him some new shoes tomorrow,' I hissed. That was the last we heard of Bishwa's mysterious disappearing shoes. The lad was crimson with embarrassment. We admire virtue but we love our friends for their failings and foibles.

Money poured in, along with the beers. Dhal produced his pipes and joyously blew away the group of awed youngsters who had brought theirs too. The pipes were always our secret, or not so secret, PR weapon. They are, above all, manifest confirmation of our two countries' links. As someone who had piped at the Queen Mother's 100th birthday parade just the week before, Dhal was practically royal himself. Always ready with a room-lighting smile, Dhal's face took on a special faraway look when piping as if this was a serious business which did not invite levity. One of the most gifted pipers I know, he also had a lungpower that could transform the great Highland pipe into a snarling instrument of war, curdle the blood and incite martial acts of crazed violence. Let's not forget, it's for this property alone that pipers are employed in the military. Dhal was not just bloody loud, his massive high altitude lungs could ensure the notes held true as well. Dhal made the youngsters sound like flautists taking their first gentle puffs. The applause was rafter-shaking stuff. The beers formed ripples and the ashtrays jumped.

The bonhomie greased the clock and when Provost Ronnie Johnstone presented us with a photo album published to mark the town's 400th anniversary, he also asked what the hell we were doing here past midnight.

Dhal and I were sitting together, full of drink, laughing and joking, but had to admit that the Provost had a point. The explanation that we needed to relax and unwind after the long day didn't really wash when the relaxation and unwinding was taken to such an extreme. Ah, well, I went to bed happy again.

Overleaf. ***Left:*** **Gyan took photos very seriously and always adopted a cobra-like look of intensity as befitting a man in his position: our senior NCO.** ***Right:*** **The east-bound traveller leaves Sanquhar by a long slow climb.**

GURKHA REIVER

V

Sanquhar to Beattock

~~~

A blister had initially formed on his right foot. He'd then favoured the left which then grew an ulcer of its own. Both feet were now sources of pain. The twenty-eight mile walk to Beattock was beyond Gyan today. My trust in his opinion was total. As he stood, brown face grim in the rain, imparting the news in his usual factual way, I was grateful for the deadpan honesty. The team came first. He'd see a doctor that morning. For all we knew, he'd never rejoin us. It was a terrible blow.

I knew from the moment we first shook hands that Gyan, with his quietly serious expression but explosive laugh, was going to be a friend for life. A group of six Gurkhas had met up to cycle round Scotland two years before and we introduced ourselves by giving background details on our lives. When it came to my turn I announced that I had been at school with Tony Blair which brought a comic look of disbelief from Gyan, whose eyes bulged with incredulity.

'*The* Tony Blair, the Prime Minister?'

'Er, yes. I knew him quite well, when he had a big Afro hair-do. He was never a prefect,' I confided,' Not like …' I pointed confidentially to my swelling chest. There was a roar of laughter.

It isn't exactly an achievement to have gone to school with someone who later came to be famous, although it can be of interest. I once wrote an article entitled: 'Prime Ministers I knew at school.' Furthermore, my background came in handy when an Austrian named Gunther whom I met on a Greek island kept telling everyone how he had been at school with Arnold Schwarzenegger – as if Arnie's fame and pulling power had somehow rubbed off on him. I couldn't resist. It was, he complained, the first time he'd been out-schoolfriended.

Gyan's career was at that tricky stage which required promotion from staff sergeant to sergeant major in order to stay in the Gurkhas. Unlike Corporals Dhal and Kali, he was senior enough to have his wife
~~~

and kids here in the UK. It was typical of him and his clan to accept his lot. 'If I'm promoted, good. If not, I leave,' he declared. 'Jey hola hola.' The phrase means 'whatever will be will be' and is heard a lot, reflecting Gurkha fatalism, along with 'It must have been written that I go so far and no further.' A conclusion applied to life's every set back.

Gyan, despite the acquiescence, was a cool thoughtful man with a fine brain. His handwriting was beautiful and his English colloquial, unlike Kali, whose grasp of English was deceptively bad. Kali had fooled me with his habit of repeating my last few words, implying a non-existent comprehension. If told: 'Don't go over there where the heather becomes boggy, it's too dangerous.' Kali would apparently agree, beaming: 'It's too dangerous.' Only when he headed for said boggy heather did it dawn that he'd never understood the warning at all. With Gyan, the possibility of misunderstanding never crossed my mind. He would have given the warning in the first place.

His concern for the men was endearing. This interest also extended to his own welfare in a manner that could be anything from understandable to downright infuriating. His inborn pessimism permitted flights of fancy beyond the ken of most and it was always Gyan who cautioned against bizarre disaster scenarios involving the improbable. He, of course, would consider that he had simply covered all the angles. These managed to include, in just this one trip, failing torch batteries, unsecured straps or other fantastic catastrophes that told you he hadn't just thought the planning through but that the outlandish was all part of his mental territory.

If you didn't have enough potential problems, Gyan would dream up some more. It was his gift to pre-planners everywhere: Cassandra with imagination.

It was Gyan, though, who created one of my permanent personal habits. He taught me to beckon Gurkha-style with fingers down, not up – a practice children especially respond to more happily and appear to find less threatening than the single finger beckon as used by authorities like cops and maths teachers.

The year before he had addressed the national conference of the British Legion and his speech had brought the house down. Admittedly, I had written it but Gyan transformed it. My heart nearly burst. This small muscular man stood in front of hundreds of curious Legionnaires, his timing perfect, drawing them in and delivering the half-funny punch-lines like a maestro. When the tumultuous applause died down, I couldn't wait to congratulate the lad.

'Shyabash, Gyan, thulo shyabash! Weren't you nervous?'

He pondered the question. 'Well, I felt a little strange,' he concluded. It dawned on me, Gurkhas have no nerves. Like that Red Indian tribe who had no fear of heights and construct skyscrapers, it was in the blood. I've never witnessed such a rapturous reception in years of attending such events. He was winning, flattering, comic and sincere. Everything in a speaker and everything in a man.

Gyan unquestionably shared his people's sense of humour. When we first knew each other there were always polite enquiries as to the health of my wife and children. This, I stupidly allowed to drag on, until eventually I had to shame-facedly inform him of my single-person style status.

There was a pause as he absorbed the astounding fact. And then the laughter detonated to a point where our friendship was threatened. My ears hurt as much as my pride. Generously, he never referred to this comedy again.

Like all Gurkhas, Gyan was fantastic with children. It's a fact, Gurkhas love kids and kids love Gurkhas. My fondest memory of Gyan was in the Highland village of Braemar when the children from the local primary, all fresh-faced and fascinated, gathered round in the High Street. Gyan, in short-sleeve combat shirt and broad felt hat, was in his element – towering over an audience at last. He didn't speak much of soldiering but of his home village, its harshness, the absence of running water, how the womenfolk laboured and how crops failed. To hear that your family could only feed itself for four months of the year was a revelation and deeply affecting for the wee ones. They all knew of Mount Everest, their teacher had done well, and were only disappointed to learn that although Gyan could see it every day, he hadn't got round to ever climbing the thing.

Nepalis call Everest 'Sagarmatha' which means 'Brow of the Sky' – although they use our name too – and have strong emotions about the peak. Sherpas, being Buddhists originally from Tibet, call it 'Chomolungma', 'Unshakable Good Elephant Woman'. To them it is the abode of the protective goddess Miyolangsangma, one of the Five Long-

Life Sisters who reside on five Himalayan peaks. Orginally a demoness, she was converted to Buddhism, and rides a tiger, holding a flower and bowl of divine food, symbolic of her inexhaustible giving. Strangely, although named after Sir George Everest in 1865, an earlier surveyor general of the Great Trigonomical Survey of India, he pronounced his name 'Eve-rest.' It had been realised that Peak XV was the world's highest in 1852 by a Bengali computer (the term given to clerks that do maths), Radhanath Sikhdar, working in Calcutta on measurements made three years before from six survey sites with twenty-four inch theodolites over a hundred miles away. He had computed, taking into consideration the earth's curvature, atmospheric refraction and plumb-line deflections, that Peak XV stood at 29,002 feet. Today's satellites tell us he was out by 26 feet – currently the accepted height is 29,028 feet or 8,848 metres. I like this story, and although only tangentially relevant, I make no apologies for its inclusion.

My friendship with Gyan had been forged on a GWT fundraiser where circumstances were not as relaxed as Gurkha Reiver. Every day had thrown up problems, disasters and personality conflicts which didn't always make for harmony. In the face of this, Gyan and I became firm allies and when we parted his earnest 'Keep in touch' had been taken to heart.

Today though, on Day 5 of our trek, it was like leaving him behind in the Sanquhar jungle with just a waterbottle and box of ammo. I had no doubt that if I'd told him to, he'd have shot anyone on our trail with grim passivity until the ammo was gone, before rising, kukri in hand, to take on anyone else. Fortunately such circumstances are rare, even in southern Scotland and the scenario was not to be. The publicity would have been sensational!

Patting Gyan's shoulder in sympathy, the Reivers trooped out from their B&B into heavy drizzle made worse by the roaring engines and spray of passing juggernauts on the A76, where the Provost himself saw us off. We were impressed. 'You should see this place during Riding the Marches,' he said.

I was surprised: 'You Ride the Marches here? I thought that was strictly Borders stuff.' Mr Johnstone chuckled in his municipally-wise way and wagged his civic head delightedly. Perhaps this was the most westerly Riding in Scotland, but either way it indicated that we had hit another new cultural force, one that was gratifyingly eastern.

Our shepherd, Charles Weir, guided us to the town's edge which took us under a bridge where we came across a blind old man sheltering from the rain who had been waiting for us. This was someone with little to give away, but his face shone with the dignity of a king. He held out a single shaking pound note which could not have been more gratefully received if it were £1,000. We were deeply moved. It was more than a moment of poignancy; it was near spiritual.

The Way took a steep but extended rise past some benches which in summer doubtless provide a place for old age loafers to chew the cud, smoke a pipe or two and take in the view of the town. My legs were cold and stiff, the muscles and tendons straining unhappily. I felt neither fit nor ready to face a long day's hike and the grim weather was providing no encouragement. I suspected the shepherd was casting an eye over me with serious misgivings. Coming down from the hills yesterday we could see the Lowther Hills ahead, rising like a glorious challenge. Unmissable was the enormous white radar dome atop the highest. And guess what? We had to be up there by lunch.

We all knew that today's march, apart from being one of the longest at twenty-eight miles, took us across the roof of the Southern Upland Way, with the dome, at 720 metres, the very pinnacle. Everything to date had been preparation for this, when the land suddenly buckled and bulged, growing in height, dimensions and wildness. Crack today, though, and the back was broken.

But to guys from the Himalayas it was just a cheerful matter of taking one step at a time. First was a plateau where our shepherd said goodbye. We crossed peat hags before hitting higher rugged slopes. The weather then closed in, clouds lowered and wet squalls smacked our cheeks as the climbing continued through rough little passes where the surrounding hills showed rips of erosion and where sprawling scree streamed between tousled heather, the first time we'd come across the plant.

'You know what? In Edinburgh there are health clubs where people spend hundred of pounds a year to use walking machines!' I commented, wiping tears of rain water from my chin.

The lads guffawed but Kali seemed wonder-struck: 'In Scotland?

Why?'

My phone rang. A journalist wanted to join us for a day. My immediate reaction was negative – too many had wanted to walk with the Gurkhas as if this were swimming with the dolphins or something. Requests had come from fell-runners, retired soldiers, school parties, and anyone else, it seemed, who was a bit bored that day. I was agin guests. Not only would they slow us down but they would diminish the oneness of the team. This journalist, however, from *The Border Telegraph* in Galashiels, seemed different: an experienced hillwalker and possibly able to help the fundraising. We agreed to meet for part of Friday.

We descended into a long rainy valley, and on to an empty derelict road, pitted with rain-dashed puddles. The scenery was changing more often than we were. The hillsides were scarred and pocked with old mines and abandoned furnaces. We were entering Scotland's highest village, Wanlockhead, where minerals had been extracted from beneath the ground since before the Romans. It was clear that the activities had been large scale with little regard for landscaping. Huge forgotten banks of crumbling brickwork rose and tumbled in rotting mystery, their purpose long unknown – unsightly messages from the past.

'This place is a famous mining town, lead and gold, but the mines are all exhausted these days,' I explained. 'In fact the Scottish crown has gold from these hills.'

As a young soldier I had survived various courses in the mountains of central Wales where similar forsaken villages, albeit slate communities, were falling into lonely disrepair. This was exactly the same. Doors and window frames were thirsty for paint and the little streets were bare of people. There was, too, the same silent cry of pain of a community that had bled to death.

The Reivers had crashed across eight miles in just over two hours and it was no surprise that Campbell and Keith had not anticipated our early arrival. 'I saw the green jackets going past the window and thought, that looks like our lot.' Campbell greeted, grinning in welcome beneath tousled but dry hair. Ours, of course, was slick with rain. The stall had

Overleaf. ***Left:*** **Wanlockhead nestles in its valley. We had come from the far left.** ***Right:*** **Kali looking fit and comfortable.**

been set up in the cafe of the Mining Museum but though overrun with school kids, it wasn't bringing in a lot of cash. Gyan had seen a doctor and was certainly out of the walking for the next day but, as a public relations natural, he would be extremely effective when the stall was sited in a better location, such as in Moffat that afternoon.

There was just time for a nasty cup of Kenco before filing a story to *The Scotsman* from the manager's office. The radar dome above us wiped out not just mobiles but even the domestic cordless ones too – it had to be a land line.

The manager, who had been accommodating already, had written, the week before, a letter for *The Scotsman* which I was quick to praise. Guess what: I could use his phone! Simon Pia took down the details of Joanna Lumley's involvement, delighted to hear that her London address was Albert Square. The eventual piece asked whether she could take over from Peggy at the Old Vic.

The path out led steeply, very steeply, upwards into a brightening sky, but first we stopped at what looked like a water-filled horse trough to find enthusiastically noisy kids determinedly panning for gold like this was the Yukon in its prime.

'Any luck?' we asked, to be shown water-filled test tubes swirling with flakes of gold. The children's happy grins implied they were on the very verge of hitting the jackpot and retiring to a country estate complete with expensive cars and grovelling servants. The excitement this engendered among our lads threatened any further progress that day. The very idea that gold was here for the taking seemed fabulous and, of course, it is. Put it this way, no one was much interested in the big beam engine, a monstrous pump which was once used to drain the nearby mine and features in much promotional literature. Who cares about an old pump, thought the guys, when there's gold in these here hills!

'When I win the lottery I will buy a house in Scotland, over in the west, near Stranraer, but I will come here often,' announced Dhal importantly. His English was very good but when excited the pronunciation faltered. It fell to bits today.

Then it was time to go, across some rough ground, briefly up the road and then up through the heather to the looming peak. I was as psychologically prepared for this as if it had been a summit attempt upon

Everest itself. It was hard work and a wind had blown up too, but helpfully behind us. Dhal's big chest occasionally swivelled to check we were still with him, but, although putting in a good effort myself, I was sure that Kali and Bishwa's presence behind me was entirely diplomatic. The two were sauntering, I knew.

At last we reached the blasted dome. The high spot of the entire march. All downhill now, you know. The rain had stopped but it seemed that we were about to bump our heads on the scudding clouds. The guidebook helpfully pointed out that not only had we now briefly left Dumfries & Galloway for South Lanarkshire but that the summit used to be the burial spot for the area's suicides. How bloody appropriate, I thought, but then tried to picture the struggle by a gaggle of stocky wee Borderers to bring a coffin all the way up here, the highest spot in the land. They must have been tough in those days. A bunch of Dragoons had been ambushed in the plunging Enterkin valley to our west, and the Covenanter prisoners released. Prince Charlie's army had retreated along this way too. How misleadingly quiet it seemed now, I thought.

On the dome's lee side we stopped for a snack, careful to prevent the wind blowing away our crisps but Bishwa chose the moment to produce his video camera. Like some windswept BBC correspondent reporting from one of the world's hotspots, I stood blethering into his lens, pronouncing heroically on the Scots regard for the Gurkhas and how this was all bringing us together. High-minded stuff, but what else could I say? The playback showed regular snowfalls, produced, I suppose, from the radar sweep. At no time in the planning stages for Gurkha Reiver did I ever envisage myself making recordings on top of mountains, far less under what appeared to be a snow shower.

'Okay, guys! All downhill to Moffat!' Everything went according to plan for about ten minutes. The weather cleared and we hurried round the curved ridgeline before realising that ahead of us lay a whole series of hills, each slightly smaller than Lowther Hill but every one requiring a steep climb. This was horrifying and not what I'd just promised. Laid out like a row of humpbacked whales, the map was practically brown with wriggling contours. 'All downhill, eh?' giggled Dhal, his lean face creased in smiles.

There was unexpected excitement on the second descent when a big ram, taking fright, tried to leap through a hole in the adjacent fence but instead angrily entangled its horns in the wire. The boys reacted instantly and without word or warning charged forward howling. My own senses exploded in excitement, and found myself galloping forward too.

Dhal accelerated into a rugby tackle, hands around the animal's neck, its muddy fleece flapping in fear. Kali grabbed a flailing back leg while I dived at the other, oblivious to a possible kick in the face. The ram, a moment ago angrily frustrated, was now panic stricken, as three of us crashed into it, our joint impact whacking the breath from its lungs.

Bishwa quickly pulled the wire away from the horns and within seconds the animal's great woolly body charged forward through the hole like a truculent bulldozer in top gear. It stopped briefly, turning a blazing eye upon us before shooting over the crest. We couldn't stop ourselves – we laughed and laughed until we too had no breath left. The whole thing had been over in seconds but had come about entirely through instinct. It had been an exhilarating, hilarious act of unity. By myself I'd have fretted for ten minutes gingerly attempting to free the beast and probably failing. Not today! Not with this lot!

This incident had a geographical dimension too. The fence marked a border. The ram had bolted from South Lanark into Dumfries & Galloway.

We carried on down the hill, grouse lifting loudly from thick heather, bright brown against the sunlit purple, until we hit a climb so spectacularly steep I could actually feel my heart sink. It had the comic dimensions of something from *Road Runner*. An anvil might fall on my head at any moment. I began trudging up in bottom gear. The others skipped past. Suddenly, my pack was a serious burden. Steps became slow and laboured. I thought about those daft people that pay good money to use exercise bikes, and why there's never a taxi when you want one.

'C'mon, Neil, is easy. You can do it!' said Kali, grinning by my side.

'Yeah,' I gasped, 'right up to the first false horizon.'

'Yes!' Kali agreed with innocent enthusiasm, swinging an arm in encouragement. Somehow my steps kept coming and the moment passed. Please, Kali, all I ask is just don't start singing. This is tough enough without complete humiliation as well. My steps grew childishly small up the muddy tussocks but somehow never stopped. Later I was to remember this hill as the most difficult of the trip but I will also never forget Kali's pleasure that I kept going.

Then I made another terrible map-reading error, or as I prefer to call it, an entirely understandable misreading of the route. Instead of being about to tumble down the next shoulder, there in front of us loomed another unfeasibly mammoth climb. 'Where the bloody hell did that come from?' I looked askance: 'That shouldn't be there!' Remonstrating with the map, I realised, of course, it showed the height figures rising not declining. I had the map at the wrong angle too; we were not heading north, but north east. Infuriated that I had made such an elementary mistake, I howled in frustration. But the thing had to be done – and it was.

The row of five summits, a chain of peaks, each horribly high, stretched ahead separated by plunging gorges, but by now I was in gear. And, all this exercise would make me fit and attractive to women, wouldn't it? Check out my thighs, girls. Tom Cruise would probably pay a fortune to go through all this.

Eventually there was a steep descent, a two-hundred metre drop in half a kilometre in fact – and that *is* steep, believe you me – to the A702 that followed the valley floor where possibly the world's only snaking Roman road ran alongside. If going the other way, east to west, the drop would have been a horrible climb before having to hit the main peaks.

The hot sun invited it and our progress deserved it. We settled down by the road for a leisurely snack. The clean red tarmac of the A702, flat and straight, was a man-made intrusion out here and surprisingly alien, I thought. Not so, to Kali at least, who à propos nothing, pointed happily and announced: 'This road, Neil, I know it!'

Our heads turned in surprise. What was Kali thinking of now? 'In 1998 I cycled here with Major Whitehead Sahib,' he averred. Nodding, I thought it just possible, before reverting to catching some rays, coffee and a smoke. I discovered later that Kali had never in his life been in this valley. The nearest had been slightly north of Dumfries – miles away.

The route then took us across the Potrail Water, through the dark Watermeetings Forest and then, having swept round the huge Daer Reservoir, on a contour of Hoda Hill in hot sun, we stopped for a quick

Overleaf. ***Left:*** **Like all Gurkhas, Dhal was a PR natural. Here, on an earlier trip, he raises a laugh from an otherwise shy drummer girl.** ***Right:*** **Women of all ages, it seems, like a Gurkha.**

MIN

cuppa at about 4 p.m., overlooking the calm expanse of water. The landscape was changing yet again. This was one of the last 'lakes' we would see. As the source of the River Clyde, it was an indication as to how far we had come. There is a spot in Watermeetings Forest that is the exact half-way mark of the whole Southern Upland Way. It wasn't far enough though, I phoned Paddy to explain we might be late. There was a moment's silence: 'The whole of Moffat is waiting for you in the High Street. Try your best to be on time.' His voice was completely sincere, the intonation without accusation, but I knew what had to be done. Again my heart sank. The whole of Moffat? This I must see. Furthermore, as if to add to our woes, the route now went, irritatingly, almost due south.

Now was the time for all good men to bite the bullet. Ten miles of difficult terrain in two hours. Five miles an hour is a so-so jogging speed, giving a four-and-a-half-hour Marathon time, but this was over a tough course and carrying packs. I explained the situation to the four earnest faces who nodded in comprehension. The gauntlet was picked up. Our pace became heated, even angry, as the route took us around an immense unnamed forest whose edges trimmed the horizons for miles. We charged over a stile as if under fire and into the plantation, re-entering Dumfries & Galloway, and found ourselves at the very top of a five mile staircase-like firebreak. Despite our thumping pace, we were still behind schedule. Something had to be done.

'Right. guys,' I told the crew. 'We're gonna jog down here. Fasten your jholas [packs] because this is going to be sore.' My knees had been increasingly painful. My feet had taken a pounding. The only escape from these aches was climbing uphill, but now we were going to trot downhill – for an unspecified period.

Boy, did we run! Hands on *jhola* straps, we went on and on, leaping like heavy-weight deer but never abandoning a steady near-suicidal charge. As pines and pink foxgloves blurred past it occurred to me that few Southern Upland Way walkers could have done it quite like this.

We stopped twice for about ten seconds to halt momentum accelerating into outright madness, and the boys were right on my heels. Our speed was asking for an accident and it was important we didn't lose control. Down and down we went until, at last, the land flattened, and then rose unexpectedly.

'Jesus Christ! Look at that!' I bawled, pointing to Craig Hill before us, which at 360 metres looked to me like the north face of the Eiger.

'It's just a gentle gradient,' said Bishwa soothingly as we stared at the slope.

'Yes, but it's up-bloody-hill!' Trust Bishwa, never spoke all day and then uses an inflammatory phrase straight from a map-reading class. The man must be a psychiatrist. Then it occurred to me that whenever faced with an unexpected physical challenge, it was only me that howled and blubbed. Better shape up, Griffiths.

Later, much later, the white van, emblazoned with the words 'Gurkha Reiver' and crossed kukris, came into view like a welcome ambulance. We piled in like helicopter-extracted troops leaving a still-dangerous battle zone. Campbell drove us to Moffat, a couple of miles off the Way, where the locals by all accounts were awaiting us in a frenzy of excitement. We were dropped half a mile from the reception committee and the Reivers suddenly hit the Gurkha 140 pace per minute speed. A number of pensioners attempted to join us but they couldn't keep up. After what we'd been through I had no intention of accommodating anyone, least of all a bunch of hangers-on.

The van came alongside with Gyan asking for us to slow down but I was having none of it. The boys started giggling. Had the old folk but known it, they had given us a tremendous morale boost. Bishwa, Kali and Dhal wanted to go even faster and really burn them off.

One entire side of Moffat's High Street had been closed off for us. We hammered right up to the Stone Ram, the street's main focus, where several worthies awaited with an outsize cheque and hundreds of well-wishers. At that moment I wasn't tired at all, only flabbergasted. I was also extremely embarrassed by a man with a bullhorn and loud Kensington drawl who had tracked us in his car for the last bit, repeatedly bellowing: 'Give a char, the Gurkhas are har!'

We were out of the outback and back in the fundraising world of handshakes and smiles. I gave a speech to what did indeed seem like half the population of Moffat. Campbell had been right. The joke about Gurkhas and Scots being very close – the tartan, the pipes and the habit of chopping up our neighbours with either claymores or kukris – fell a little flat, but Gyan made up for it with his usual integrity. In the evening sun, while our pictures were being taken for the local press, I wondered how many had today met a Gurkha for the very first time. The local school had made a life-size papier mâché Gurkha for which I had sent the necessary photos, but the kids now seemed half fascinated and half terrified (the chopping up neighbour joke had caused a group intake of breath). Gyan was always superb when it came to pressing the flesh but the others were far too shy to do anything other than smile. The *Moffat News* was to give us a good spread with the Reivers on their haunches before a row of British Legion benefactors. I was not described as anything at all, merely: 'Neil Griffiths explained to the crowd what the Appeal was all about.' Not even as an MP. Things were slipping.

There was a handful of individuals more demanding than the others who insisted that we check out photos of Dad's time in India, but this was part and parcel of the process. I was asked by a guy aged about twenty, his girlfriend shushing him, why I didn't look like a Gurkha, Sherpa Tensing perhaps. Fatigue was sweeping over me, and my good humour was ebbing. Not at my best, I explained that I wasn't a Gurkha, I was British and the whole idea of the alliance with the Gurkhas is that we work together. I suspect my answer was made with the same lack of manners as his question. The town gave us over £1,500 in one big cheque while Keith had amassed a fortune in other donations and takings. Phew! Worth visiting!

We were accommodated together in a splendid B&B, a former manse so immense it once had its own chapel. The rooms spoke of modern expenditure with just the right touch of antiquity. Our boots made a filthily friendly heap by the front door and our stained jackets and *jholas* decked the hall. The couple who ran it were simply superb. Our laundry was done without a quibble and chocolate bars were donated. Kali learned that the lady of the house was from Norfolk and surprised us by solemnly announcing he knew the place. Norfolk? It was where all the contestants from *Blind Date* come from he claimed. 'I know this, I have seen it on television,' he nodded sagely to a blank look from the lady in question. When we discovered that the man of the house was, in fact, a widower and that the lady was his employee, we cheered for the two kids who lived in such a wonderful place and blessed them all.

In the adjacent cemetery lay our nemesis, John Loudon McAdam, the creator of the road surface destined to hammer the feet of our little group nearly two hundred years after its introduction. As a matter of fact, his crushed stone layer technique was first used in 1815 – the year the Gurkhas started serving the British.

With feet and faces blazing we met up with the locals again for supper but they were, as it turned out, the only group on the whole trip intelligent enough to realise that, having done the PR-fundraising bit, we wanted to rest and be alone. At 8 p.m. we were left entirely by ourselves to have supper in an imposing hotel but not before the bar had collected £60 for the Gurkha Welfare Trust. My knees, half numb and half on fire, would have been only slightly more flexible had they been in plaster of Paris. I got to my feet like a veteran with gout, and then didn't like to sit down and repeat the process.

Good plentiful food was vital but the opportunity to have a Gurkha *bhat* (curry) was all too rare. A dish always livened up with *khorsani* (chilli); it is their staple. I knew from experience that there had to be at least chilli sauce if not fresh chilli in my larder when Gurkhas came to stay. Great was the astonishment the time I forgot. Two years before, finding myself in a Buckie hotel with Dhal while cycling round Scotland, he assured me that a touch of fresh *khorsani* would lift the taste of my fish and chips. Lift the roof of my mouth more like, right through the top of my head.

You never saw such a tiny bite, but the heat rose inside my mouth like a nuclear breakdown. Tears leapt from my eyes. My head raged with the invisible flames normally only associated with a leaking Zippo and then swallowing a fireball. The fish was completely ruined, and it was done in those nice breadcrumbs too. Thanks, Dhal. *Khorsani* would ruin boiled cabbage. Tonight the boys consumed fresh chilli and curry in quantities which would fell any other lads' night out, even those of Glasgow.

It was immensely gratifying once to witness a signaller from West Nepal overdo the *khorsani*. His face sort of melted and sweat spurted from his temples to huge cheers from colleagues. The drips from his nose alone used up an entire serviette, and that was before he got to the nearest tap. He ate the remainder of the meal with a tea towel in one hand.

Gurkhas are strong on monarchy, calling the Queen, *hamro Maharani*, our Queen, and their passports say they're Hindu as a politeness to the King of Nepal who reigns over the world's only Hindu kingdom. It's like saying British soldiers are Christian. When a Hindu Gurkha leaves Nepal his priest gives a special dispensation to eat anything. A rite of purification is held upon his return. It was this absence of ceremony that made a Gurkha unit so swift on the Indian subcontinent; they didn't need to stop on the march for prayers and could eat anything without fuss, unlike others who could barely work for an uninterrupted hour. Let it be known, Gurkhas will eat almost anything, and plenty of it!

To have reached Annandale was to have passed the half-way mark. This is the Great Divide of the Southern Upland Way where even the names of features change. Cleuch and linns replace fells, craigs, rigs, knowes, flows and mosses. This is where it dawns on the walker that the Way may, one day, end, and from here the magic of the Borders beckons. Geographically and culturally the east and west of lowland Scotland are uniquely different. The Annan clefts the two. But for me there was something special; from this day on the Gurkhas started calling me 'Neil Sahib'. I liked being called 'Neil Sahib' very much and if they were comfortable with it, then I was quietly delighted. Yes, Neil Sahib has a certain ring to it, befitting my station, doesn't it? I thought with quiet delight: I've arrived.

The Reivers ate their fill that night, even ordering a bag of frozen peas for Gyan's feet, before heading back to the B&B, knowing that we could take on anything. Half the maps, four of eight, could now be chucked out. We were the tops, and now I was going to sleep like one.

VI

Beattock to St Mary's Loch

~~~

The first three kilometres found us, unusually, on a country road, a proper surfaced beast, and a level one too. This was not comfortable and each early morning step juddered the knees, a reminder that not only had we been on the go for five days but another three and a half lay ahead. The Romans had used this valley and, with their normal strategic savvy, had laid the area's first road, which we crossed before entering a beech wood and passing McAdam's home, Dumcrieff House. The woods included alder, sycamore (by far our most common maple), ash (our only member of the olive tree family), lime, and horse chestnut, with oak, holly and rowan. It was like progressing – the hard way – through the Botanic Gardens beside my flat in Edinburgh.

The group was in high spirits, with only twenty-one miles to go today. Bishwa was bearing a large pack, while Dhal whistled happily to Kali's murmured songs. It is a fast section of the Way, mostly down the Ettrick Valley and after yesterday's twenty-eight miles we were due a quiet day. Soon we had climbed 200 metres under a gentle grey sky and had entered a steeply-sided conifer wood comprised of our old friends, larchpole pine and sitka spruce, while trailing an infant stream, the Cornal Burn, along a stony path.

The sky cleared into a brilliant blue and our hearts lifted higher. There was nowhere else in the world I wanted to be; bliss it was that morn to be alive and strolling along the Southern Upland Way was 'very heaven'.

We stopped for drinks on the grassy banks, spirits bubbling like the burn, when Bishwa suddenly asked, 'Who's he?' indicating, Gurkha-fashion, with his thumb.

Further up the track a shambolic figure was bumbling towards our picnic spot, an old fedora on his head. He had clearly seen us, whoever he was, and as the road dipped into dead ground, he disappeared. We waited
~~~

for him to re-appear but he stayed hidden. Either he'd stopped or left the road. What was going on? Then the hat was seen bobbing above some bushes to our right.

'Stupid man,' I said to myself: 'He's trying to creep up on us!'

Bishwa needed no prompting and, half crouching, sloped off into the trees to the target's left to outflank him, as the rest of us rolled into cover.

The stranger realised we had disappeared almost immediately and slowly straightened up, frowning in puzzlement. He gingerly stepped forward until only yards from where we lay, when Bishwa's red-shirted figure rose behind him like a Nepalese Freddy Kruger .

I looked up with a cheerful: 'Good morning!' which caused him to freeze in fright. Whipping off his hat, he held it in both hands like some yokel meeting the lord of the manor, and blurted the odd: 'Thank you, thank you very much!'

He was near palpitating in terror and for a second I felt compassion but the boys, as ever, burst out giggling.

Our man went on his way, mumbling. We were never quite sure whether he was all there. Had we taken advantage of a passing simpleton or merely frightened the wits from a nosey local? The Reivers didn't seem bothered either way. Gurkhas don't show special consideration for the disabled; they treat them as normal. One thing I did know: no one in his right mind stalks Gurkhas for fun, and if he tried, we, at least, would not be caught napping. If, like in a movie, Bishwa had actually tapped him on the shoulder, I suspect we would have had a cardiac case.

This vaguely bizarre little incident was oddly defining. No one thought it particularly strange. They enjoyed it, shrugged it off and went forward unthinkingly. It was never mentioned again. There had been an element of potential violence, but only in play, even in the way the stranger was sent off without any disrespect. This was merely the natural order by ordinary Gurkhas, those stoic, homicidal, gentlemanly gigglers: our very own Spartans. I can't imagine this scene being carried out by, say, paratroopers. The innocence would be missing.

On another trip two former British soldiers had attempted to integrate by recounting several filthy jokes as if to say: we're all lads together, aren't we? This is how some bond, but not our boys. They don't swear in normal conversation nor include parts of the anatomy to describe the weather and don't regard tattoos as macho. They are different. Nevertheless, our lads listened to the jokes with nodded smiles but without comment. The lack of reciprocation was obvious, but so too were the good manners which prevented them from offending the would-be pals. It was one of the first occasions on which I was able to interpret Gurkha passivity, but it completely by-passed the jokers.

Although not a characteristic of our team, most Gurkhas have a comical ability to invent preposterous excuses to explain away life's set-backs. One driver once told me that the road had got lost. The road? A piper (no names) was known to demur occasionally from invitations to play on the grounds that his pipes 'were too tired'. There was a famous case when a certain driver hit a steel-reinforced concrete bollard in his Land Rover. His defence? 'The bollard moved,' a fact which was repeated with increasing conviction from said driver. To save face, he was found guilty of failing to anticipate the bollard's movement.

It's tempting to patronise the Gurkhas. While their diminutive height, boyish faces, lack of guile, and sunny disposition make affection easy, their innocence of our culture can lead to a mistaken belief that their naïvety is characteristic. A rural background can make most trusting, and isolated mountain communities in the Third World more so. Still, some things are universal. I was taken aback one time to hear a Gurkha friend, not only declare his allegiance to Liverpool FC, but also to discover that he'd actually visited Anfield several times.

Time to move on. I checked our progress. On all forest roads, unless a very close eye is kept on the map, you have only a vague idea of your position. I stood up and announced the fact.

'River on left,' snapped Bishwa, as always, the earnest young soldier. Hiding a smile, I pulled out the map.

'We haven't seen a guide post for a bit. Keep your eyes open,' I requested.

'Ah, yes,' added Kali: 'Keep eyes open.'

'Ach look, there's one right there!' I pointed at the stob which was only yards away.

'Neil Sahib!' shouted Kali jubilantly: 'Look! Guide post! Dahar!'(There!)

'Yes, I know! I just told you!'

Dhal and Bishwa burst out laughing, joined by Kali, unconcerned to be the butt of the joke, only happy that we were happy.

After five miles or so we exited the forest on to a watershed. In fact, one of the great watersheds of Scotland and pivotal to our progress had we but known. On our left the Selcoth Burn fell down to the Moffat Water, which in turn flows into the Annan and Irish Sea. Only yards away was the headland of the Ettrick Water which later joins the Tweed and then the North Sea. This was no ordinary peat hag, it defined the Lowlands. The map showed 'hopes' too, a name peculiar to the east, meaning a meandering burn.

We traipsed along a contour until a fence was crossed bearing the surprising but uplifting notice: 'Welcome to the Scottish Borders.' Another milestone. Dumfries and Galloway was now behind us, never to return again. It was onward, onward. The North Sea, though, was metaphorically and literally miles away.

There was another mature conifer plantation to cross and then down to the Ettrick Water where we tramped down the Ettrick Valley on a Land Rover road, reminiscent of the long one on Tuesday beside the Scaur Water. The hills rose, bare and mighty, on either side, the road occasionally passing lonely cottages, mostly in good repair but apparently empty. The proper lived-in ones were surrounded by pecking hens and abandoned agricultural equipment. Apparently, goats indicate former schoolteachers who have dropped out to have a shot at the good life. The nanny state? No sign of Felicity Kendall look-alikes, alas. To live here you need a car and the track developed into a proper tarmacked road.

The heat became so oppressive that when we stopped for lunch the shade tempted us, but our legs, which only ached when rested, needed sun as if it were some natural deep ray therapy. Appetite had fallen away. Just coffee and chocolate bars, along with cigs. I felt drowsy, thirsty and in need of a comfy chair. My legs took several minutes to get back in gear when we re-started. An outsider would have concluded I was, at least, partially disabled.

'There was a famous author who lived along here, James Hogg, who wrote a whole load of really good books. There's a monument to him over there. He was called the Ettrick Shepherd and was very famous,' I announced like an apprentice tourist guide who can't really be bothered.

Kali was entranced: 'So, Neil Sahib, why was he called the Trick Shepherd?'

My legs were well and truly run-in by the time the route left the road and took a path which headed steeply skywards through rough grazing before traversing a rounded saddle to connect us with St Mary's Loch below. I was in the lead when a voice called down from above.

Bishwa stood stock still: 'The sahib is speaking our language!'

Not quite sure what was happening, I could see, to my amazement, Kali on my left moving up the hill like a gazelle. The speed was super human. I have never seen such acceleration. It was surreally fast. Kali raced for the summit, homing in on the voice.

The figure on the skyline was revealed and I suddenly understood what was happening. A former Gurkha officer, Major Don Whitehead, and Kali's one-time company commander, had come out to greet us with girl friend Margaret.

There was a moment of pleasure and relief. I hadn't wanted anyone not-of-us to join but Don was different and his appearance welcome. It would also preclude any later charges of exclusion too.

Kali was thrilled and as the group assembled at the top of the pass, it could have been Nepal. Nobody was using English and the welcome was both genuine and mutual.

To our left was, after another five miles, the Loch of the Lowes with St Mary's Loch almost attached to its east end but separated by an ancient alluvial landslip. The Way threaded down to the Loch below where Campbell, Gyan and Keith spotted us but couldn't work out who the fifth figure was, because as fate would have it, Don was wearing a red polo shirt almost identical to ours. I was extra-specially pleased: we had moved off the fifth of eight maps.

The descent was, for me, the first really painful one of the trip. My knees ached with an imprecise pain. They weren't swollen, just bloody sore.

At last we reached the lochs where Tibbie Sheils Inn stands, white-washed and ancient. Not only was the Way officially opened here in 1984 but it was where James Hogg met Sir Walter Scott to discuss literature. A phone mast in the adjacent field permitted A1 phone links and again I filed a story to *The Scotsman*, relieved not to have missed the deadline. Sitting down to make the call was a mistake. Rising to my feet and turning to the right brought a searing pain across the knees, a grating agony as if their bearings were being gouged. I could walk but not turn.

'How're your feet?' had been a question from the start. My reply: 'I have no idea. As far as I can tell I left them in New Luce!' True, they may have been numb from the continual battering but they recovered every night. The big blister on my right heel, strangely, never caused any pain. At this time of day, 4 p.m., my boots took on a new weight but could apparently keep walking all by themselves. I only had to stand and start them up.

Don and Margaret made their goodbyes at the edge of St Mary's Loch. The distance to the day's finish was a frustrating seven kilometres: not short enough to look after itself, and not long enough to be beyond comprehension. On the north side was the hotel in which my parents had honeymooned. I called my mum as we passed to be reminded that my dad had nearly been arrested there for fishing without permission. His explanation, that he was merely teaching his new wife to cast, was accepted with a bailiff's grin of disbelief.

It took an hour to traverse the loch and I, for one, moved tenderly when climbing into the waiting Reiver van. Kali seemed upset that we'd gone quite so fast as he'd been unable to enjoy the scenery but I was not listening. I had been clattering behind Bishwa who seemed to move ahead like a roe deer, uncatchably fleet. My legs were so numb they could have been out on loan as far as I knew. We had at least an hour's drive ahead of us and time, as always, was pressing.

Later, standing in the Border village of Newcastleton, the evening sunshine blazing, we checked into two adjacent hotels, small and cosy. An overweight, unshaven drinker pushed past.

'What ye're staring at?' he demanded.

'You!' I replied forcefully and needlessly offensive. This reaction was clearly not what Fat Man had expected, and he blinked in confusion before going on his way wordlessly. The opportunity to have my face smacked went with him. The Gurkha ethos doesn't include impetuous

Opposite: **St Mary's Loch where the Way is flat and fast.**

insult and part of me was astonished but it was drawn on a rising self-assertion. No one is going to gratuitously intimidate me, Lord of the Mountains and Friend of the Gurkhas. I was getting grandly above myself. Naïve and silly, obviously, but just a teeny bit understandable. I wondered what Gurkhas look like when they lose their tempers: probably outwardly impassive. There isn't such a phrase, 'to go Nepaleptic', though I wouldn't bank on that. Ask the Japanese.

The only time I saw tempers snap was when Dhal, in Lockerbie two years earlier, trying to reverse a caravan, was interrupted by a young Buddhist monk, and then it was more a forceful irritation as opposed to aggressive anger. The monk was probably from Europe's biggest Buddhist temple at Eskdalemuir and had foolishly attempted to thrust brochures on to Dhal who briskly informed him that not only was he already a Buddhist, but a busy corporal to boot. Never mind, Brother. That was a once in a lifetime experience – or in your case, once in every lifetime.

Newcastleton, population 880, and only miles from the Border may appear a strange choice for the Reivers, but as participants in Ayo Gurkha in '98 we knew this place was a wee gem. A single street of mellow stone beauty. It was apparently designed as a model village by a philanthropic nineteenth century owner, around a tree-filled square, now complete with war memorial. It was the type of place where, when the petrol pump goes on the blink, people talk about it for years. Yet I don't think it had anything as grand as a filling station.

The entire population enveloped us in 1998 (someone in a state of high excitement even photographed me as I jumped down from our Defender) and put on a concert in our honour. It was the hit of the trip and a place to which the boys swore they'd return. I even remembered my initial arrival at the tiny hotel: 'We've been fully booked by Gurkhas,' had been the receptionist's proud rebuff. 'I am a Gurkha!' had been my triumphant riposte. Today the same receptionist leapt from her seat to welcome us back. There was a moment to remind Dhal to have breakfast in his own hotel and not get muddled, like the last time, when he was found

Opposite: **Kali with a young Newcastleton admirer.**
Overleaf. ***Left:*** **Teddy Boy. The Bimbahadur Bear was a great seller.**
Right: **Gurkha supporters come in all ages and with all levels of enthusiasm.**

GURKHA
WELFARE
TRUST

chewing bacon and eggs next door having gone for a walk and become confused. There's no wrath like a Scottish landlady discovering she's fed an interloper.

Time, that bastard, gave us barely minutes for a coffee, a cig, a shower and a change into suits, before meeting up in the barn-sized Legion club. Gyan and I stood outside with Dhal blethering, but inside we were ticking that Bishwa and Kali had not arrived. The locals were genuinely ecstatic to see us again and accepted explanations about Kali and Bishwa's tardiness with shrugs and smiles. One lady told me proudly that she had recently changed the name of her cottage to 'Bemersyde' to honour Earl Haig of Bemersyde. Clearly, if anyone informed me that his cottage was now entitled Blenheim Palace, it would not be on grounds of self-delusion but in reverence to good old Marlborough. Oh, and incidentally, I've decided to call myself Duke – in homage, you understand. And where the bloody hell were Kali and Bishwa?

Eventually the wee rascals, their hair wet from the shower, scurried across from the hotel, hands held up in prayer-greeting. You couldn't scold. Not even Kali's flapping collar. Someone from the local paper took a whole load of photos beneath a poster I'd sent out weeks before. Later I noticed that Gyan had climbed on a step to appear taller. I smiled when the cutting came. Gyan took photos very seriously; there could never be too many and it was important that he cut a dash in each. This meant a stately, nay serious expression bordering on imperiousness, which would portray him as both worldly and wise. Group pictures always showed a happy bunch of grinning lads, teeth gleaming, while Gyan would be there taking it all in coolly, with all the gravitas one would expect of the senior NCO. Tonight though, off camera of course, Gyan was his usual high-spirited self.

We entered the building, shaking hands with a receiving committee who were of all ages but shared the same huge smile. The spirit of 1998 was back! Gurkhas like small villages because they are from small villages themselves – and the sentiment was returned tenfold. The community had turned out en masse. We had kept our promise; we were back.

The concert was a half a celebration and half a community event: a community celebration even. Two kids dressed in black sang *Kung Fu Fighter* to a backing tape, with accompanying high kicks and karate chops. One was clearly a gifted performer while his pal had obviously been suckered into the whole thing, his actions less enthusiastic and embarrassed. His voice sang the lyrics but his body shouted: 'How the hell did I get into this?' They were followed by a line dance or two by a host of gorgeous little cowgirls in stripy shirts, frills and boots – so charming and innocent you cried. One wee girl's performance would be constantly interrupted by grimly unselfconscious halts as her falling skirt was solemnly hoiked up but otherwise the scene was of whirling, stamping pride and happiness. You wondered if all this would be possible in a city and decided, probably not. Later, men played guitar to ballads, handing the instrument over to their successors or asking the grocer, publican or fellow farmhand to accompany them. A night of a thousand photos. I took one of Kali, hugging a ten-year-old cowgirl, and captured pure innocent bliss. Again, there was that sense of humble uplift, of being witness to good folk doing good.

A folded blazer, with the black Gurkha buttons, over the back of a chair, looked so small I realised I hadn't come across one in that size since I was fourteen. And yet in uniform, these guys transform into smart wee thugs whose latent threat keeps the wary at bay merely by appearance. How is this possible? 'Your reputation precedes you, good sirs,' is hardly an adequate explanation.

'When you say that the radar dome on Lowther Hill blocked your phones, you should bear in mind that radar waves are not continuous. They're not microwaves either,' chided a tweedy elderly figure. 'Another thing. You smoke!' As if this promised eternal damnation, but we were above anything. And what are radar waves made up from?

I foolishly asked the innocent question to be avoided in small rural communities: 'Is that your son?' to hoots of smothered laughter and wagging heads. My mind flashed to a similar scene in *Local Hero* and suddenly felt a whole lot less than cosmopolitan. I like comedies, I just don't like playing an unwitting part in them.

There had been apologies that some of the club's stalwarts were at a wedding and as if in compensation, the villagers began buying our raffle tickets by the armful. Charles, as Colonel-in-Chief of the Royal Gurkha Rifles, had been approached to donate a prize. 'Do you wish a signed book of water colours or a bottle of whisky from HRH's 50th birthday cask?'

we were asked. 'If you're offering both, could we have both?' I had replied. 'Nice try, but here's the book only,' came the reply, complete with Buckingham Palace postmark.

One serious wee girl growled that she didn't want a book by Prince Charles but would like to win the weekend for two in a top hotel. 'Don't worry,' I assured her: 'I can guarantee you won't win the book – and furthermore, you will definitely not win a weekend with Prince Charles!' This may (or may not) appear slightly humorous on the page but at the time it was greeted with the frostiness of a grande dame being cheeked by the plumber. First rule of begging: don't get smart with the public. Small boys gathered round another prize, a ceremonial kukri, asking in wonder if they won would they really be allowed to keep it. 'I could give my brother a real surprise with one of those,' claimed one wee thug, in true Border reiver style.

Eventually Newcastleton with their ticket rush were to provide four of the six winners and a guy drove up to my office in Edinburgh to pick up the prizes. Serendipity or synchronicity, I don't know, but he spotted the picture of Kali with the cowgirl. 'That's my daughter!' he exclaimed delightedly. Of course, I gave it to him.

My evening speech hit a top note by quoting part of a poem written by a First World War Gurkha officer:

Bravest of the brave,
Most generous of the generous,
Never had country more faithful friends than you ...

'and if you don't believe that then you shouldn't be here tonight.' The applause was stupendous. I was taken aback but also took aboard a new lesson: use that one again, pal.

It was here in Newcastleton two years ago that I had discovered that Gyan was an effective public speaker when he delivered a story about how the Legion plaque he'd just received would hang on the wall in a special Gurkha family centre near Nuneaton and serve to remind of this wonder-

Opposite: **Small boys hopeful they might win a raffle-prize kukri. 'I could give my brother a real surprise with one of these!' one remarked.**

ful evening. While I have reason to believe this promise was never actually fulfilled, the intent was sincere. Gyan's English, although slow, was not awkward and the impact was doubly effective. The message was not just clear, it was honest. The horrible pronunciation (Warwickshire, for instance) merely added to the impression. Tonight, he was on top form and produced the presentation Gurkha teddy bear with the flourish of a vaudeville veteran, bringing a hail of applause.

I, for one, was out of there by midnight but first we'd given a little song ourselves, led by Gyan, with the rest of us clapping and joining in on the chorus – which appeared to comprise only the words 'Jam, jam, jama jam' (brought the house down, my dears!) and was followed by a free-for-all Auld Lang Syne, grins, cheers and self-satisfied applause. It had been a tremendous night and waves of achievement and old-fashioned happiness swept through me. But we were tired and trooped off to bed as soon as was polite. Newcastleton had been an oasis of whose waters we drank deep and gratefully.

I wondered, for not the first time, how long the adrenalin created by this entire adventure would last. Somehow my legs weren't even sore any more. My mind, however, slowly drifted and then closed down.

VII

St Mary's Loch to Galashiels

Friday dawned with the sun's fingers poking through a mild grey sky, and as the van wended north to our drop-off it passed several woollen mills which brought cries of anguish from Gyan and Kali who wanted tartan gifts at factory prices but were faced with the fact that at 7.30 a.m. none were open.

'Factory prices are the best,' repeated Gyan emphatically, slapping his knee. Nepalese music played loudly on the vehicle's tape player, drowning his words with songs of woe, an apt accompaniment. Every Gurkha trip to Scotland features a frantic but discerning hunt for things tartan, from spectacle cases and scarves to purses and belts. All things you can use, but never ornaments or tartan dolls. But Gurkhas, from a barter and haggle culture, are loath to pay top dollar in an Edinburgh gift shop and all advice from experienced colleagues is to shop around.

Disembarkation was never cheery and today was the usual unemotional acceptance of our unusual existence. The team's only concern was walking, one foot in front of the other, and to make it as much fun as possible. The planet's great mysteries would have to wait until at least Sunday evening. Our march was now routine, absorbing and uplifting. The traipse never became a trudge, despite the 140 miles already gone, and there was never a case of: 'This is Thursday. It must be Gala, whirled without end, Amen.' Perhaps the journey, at a speed that was literally natural, could not blur the place and time concept. We were here, at this spot, because our feet brought us here. It might have been an idea to have installed a map of the route in the van so that our progress could be put in context, but it wasn't needed. Somewhere in our primeval heads we knew where we stood, thanks to internal global-positioning systems.

The pace was steady, with the group glad to have Gyan back, but the sun had not returned, and for the first time since Wanlockhead, we were back in green rain jackets. Embroidered sweatshirts lurked in our *jholas* should the breeze grow but though it threatened, the rain never came. Trees were left behind as the route climbed to present another huge horizon dominated by the distant Moorfoots and on the right, the bald pates of Minch Moor rose above their wooded shoulders – *gunongs*. I don't suppose I'll see such a feature again without smiling wistfully and saying the word to myself. By the time Traquair was reached we had passed only two hills but six rigs, four laws and fourteeen kilometres. The undemanding nature of the day's walk, albeit twenty-five miles, had not necessitated the customary master race speed. In fact, for the first time since Portpatrick we were actually strolling, and with Gyan and Dhal with walking sticks, the image of a gentle promenade was further enhanced.

A couple of hours later we exited the Traquair forest on what is now a footpath but once was the historic Minch Moor Road which in its time saw the royal progress of Edward I on his way to earn his title as Hammer of the Scots. There was the excitement of the Cheese Well too, a spring, where according to tradition we should have left cheese or other foodstuffs for the fairies. The guys looked askance at this information as if wondering just how gullible Scots were. We were back in open country.

It wasn't long before our party bumped into a small curly-haired walker, aged about fifty, who introduced himself as Atholl Innes of *The Border Telegraph* who was clearly taken aback at how far we had come. We shook hands and the memory of the phone call days ago jumped back.

His presence immediately brought on a polite slowing down and a silence born of shyness. Gone was the sky-ripping laughter and motorcade pace; we were with someone from civilisation now. Almost immediately, the day's highest spot (a surprising 524 metres) atop the unimaginatively named Brown Knowe, signalled a slow descent into Galashiels, ten easy miles away.

Atholl and I knew absolutely nothing about each other. His experience of Gurkhas was nil while my knowledge of the Scottish Borders was woefully thin. At least we had mutual journalist friends, and for me to have a real travel guide, instead of forever pretending to be one, was welcome. I gave the full brief on the whys and wherefores of the trip and how four boys from Nepal came to be wandering through the lush Border country of Scotland.

It's a long but unequalled story. In 1814 the British declared war on Nepal. The East India Company was spreading northwards while the vast bulk of the Himalayas dictated Nepalese expansion could only be southwards. A clash of the titans was inevitable. The British sent in four columns to have two rudely checked by outnumbered Gurkhas – who were so named because the capital was then 'Gorkha'. The British had their eyes opened and were so impressed they did something that they had never done before or since. They erected an obelisk in honour of their adversary. 'They fought in fair conflict like men, and in the intervals of actual combat, showed us liberal courtesy,' wrote a witness. The mutual appreciation society was founded on contact: love at first sight.

A Captain Hearsey wrote of them: 'They are armed with a musket with or without a bayonet, a sword, and stuck in their girdles is a crooked instrument called a kookuree ... they are very hardy, endure privations, and are very obedient,' before adding with searing prescience: 'Under our Government they would make excellent soldiers.' He wasn't a lone voice. General Sir David Ochterlony had spotted their potential and, novelly, had recommended their enlistment during the actual conflict.

A Lt Frederick Young had been instructed to take 3,000 regulars to engage a Gurkha force of just 200 but upon attack his men had fled, leaving Young and a handful of officers to be quickly surrounded by gleeful but puzzled Gurkhas. One asked why he had not run off.

'I have not come so far in order to run away,' he replied with an elan to die for.

'We could serve under men like you,' observed their leader with prophetic insight. This story only comes to us through his daughter, a Mrs Jenkins, who wrote it at an advanced age while announcing she had no family records to draw on. So, it's probably not quite true, as they say, but has a wonderful ring to it all the same, which is perhaps why it has remained with us. Young was held as an honoured prisoner and upon release, asked to form a corps of Gurkhas. This became the Sirmoor

Overleaf. ***Left:*** **Before his regiment amalgamated with 10th Gurkha Rifles to form the 2nd Royal Gurkha Rifles, Kali was a member of the 7th Gurkha Rifles. Gyan points to his old 7GR tracksuit badge.** ***Right:*** **Kids love Gurkhas and Gurkhas love kids. Children were never tense. Here Kali proves the point.**

GURKHA
WELFARE
TRUST

Battalion, which was later to change its name to the 2nd Goorkha Rifles. From such a birth sprang the alliance of trust and affection we know today. A treaty was signed in May 1815. Nepal was never a colony but hosted one of those remarkable figures of Empire – the British Resident. Clause 5 of the Convention provided for recruitment of *volunteers* from the Gorkhali western district. It was the 2nd Goorkha Rifles (they alone have this special spelling, and are also known as 'God's Own Goorkhas') that so famously took the Heights of Dargai with the Gordon Highlanders in 1897 when Piper Findlater won the Victoria Cross. A painting of the Gurkhas and Gordons attacking Kandahar in 1872 hangs in The Highlanders officers' mess (the Gordons' direct descendants) to this day.

One observer wrote: 'The genuine Goorka is recognised by his high cheek-bones, broad Tartar features. Considerably below the average height of the natives of Hindustan, broad-chested and bull-necked, with muscles of the thigh and leg greatly developed ... capable of enduring great fatigue ... perform journeys almost incredible to Europeans.' I swear he had met our lot.

Two of the best books ever on these men were *Bugles and a Tiger* and *A Child at Arms* by John Masters and Patrick Davis respectively. The first concerns the 1930s wars on the North West Frontier against the Pathans and the second describes the WWII Burma campaign. Their soldiering may have differed but not their soldiers. John Masters wrote of how his men looked him in the eye and regarded him as lucky to have them under his command.

Patrick Davis spoke about the same thing but added that while the Gurkha soldier regarded himself as an equal, the hill boy was probably superior. That these were the words of men who knew Gurkhas as well as anyone on the planet, and that their sentiments almost overlap word for word with the early 19th century descriptions, implies a level of characteristic steadfastness. Both emphasise how Johnny Gurkha (so-named because originally they were employees of the East India Company, John Company) is in thrall to no man. Once such men trust you, their loyalty compels returned trust or the whole game is off.

During the Indian Mutiny the Gurkhas unquestionably saved the Raj and forged a chain of total trust. From then on, unlike other troops of the Indian Army, any Gurkha would be welcome in a British mess and still is.

At the siege of Lucknow a mixed group of Gurkhas and Brits found themselves facing overwhelming odds but this didn't stop one sergeant coming round one evening to ask his officer if he and his men could have at least one sally soon, otherwise the plains' people would think them scared. 'I told him there would be plenty of opportunity and our little friend went away very happy,' wrote the officer. This image always puts me in mind of Gyan taking me aside and asking the same thing with the same terrifying gentleness and quiet logic.

In the First World War the Gurkhas were thrown, almost as an after thought, into the Western Front, as well as Mesopotamia, Persia, Gallipoli, Salonica and Palestine. They lost 10,000 men. Everywhere they went the reputation was burnished. In the Second World War the twenty battalions were expanded to forty-five and 250,000 men poured down from the Himalayas to fight in North Africa, Burma, Italy and Greece. Their king had allowed Britain the pick of his country – which wasn't even a colony. The legend was reaffirmed.

If ever there was a chapter more in need of remembrance it was their forgotten but stubborn refusal as Jap POWs to submit to their cruel captors. Despite bribery, indoctrination and beatings, they even refused to sign for Red Cross parcels. After four years of treatment more bestial (they were seen as race traitors) than anything meted out to Europeans, a Gurkha colonel who saw them in a POW camp after the Japanese surrender wrote:

'A wonderful sight, all scrupulously clean and neatly dressed ... To my amazement they marched as smartly as on a peacetime ceremonial.' The Gurkhas had kept the faith.

The immediate post-war period saw uncertainty. In 1946 and the partition of India looming, the Viceroy, General Wavell, realised that with National Service at only twelve months, it would be too expensive to send British conscripts to the Far East. He recommended that the Gurkhas be taken out of the Indian Army and be transferred to the British. Unfortunately, this was done far too late in the day (literally giving just a couple of weeks) and although four of the ten regiments of two battalions each were indeed transferred, there was a period when the British were not able to guarantee employment to either commissioned officers or NCOs. The Indian Government, on the other hand, promised generous bonuses.

Consequently the numbers volunteering to stay with the British were low, but all the same, recruits still came aplenty.

Insensitive blunderings aside, the newly-created British Brigade of Gurkhas found itself based in Malaya in 1947, and ideally suited to the jungle war that began the following year and lasted until 1960. Similarly, it suited the conflict with Indonesia in Borneo. Their smart work at the invasion of Brunei, in December 1962, saved the Sultan who has paid for a British Gurkha battalion to be located there ever since.

Despite the kingdom's close relations with the UK it took until 1957 for recruiting depots to be established in Nepal and until 1961 for the first battalion to be stationed in England. There are now 3,500 Gurkhas in the British Army, two battalions of the newly-formed Royal Gurkha Rifles, plus the ancillary corps, signals and engineers, while three British infantry regiments have a Gurkha support company. There are two Gurkha Demonstration Companies, one at Brecon and the other at Sandhurst of course, whence came Cpl Kali, late of the 7th Gurkha Rifles, and Rfn Bishwa, late of the 10th Gurkha Rifles.

The Gurkha Welfare Trust is mostly interested in the 12,000 surviving wartime Gurkhas who, by serving for only a few years instead of a full fifteen, receive no pension from anyone, least of all their own country which is far too poor to fund a welfare state. While the Ministry of Defence pays proper pensions to 25,000 Gurkhas who fulfilled the full term of duty, it also pays the Trust's administration costs in Nepal.

Every Gurkha is proud to donate a day's pay per annum and joyfully participates in any other fundraising ventures which will benefit his glorious forebears. Coming from a community where elders are revered this should not be surprising, and trusted old soldiers run a careful intelligence net in Nepal with twenty-four welfare centres providing education and health care. Bridge-building and freshwater schemes have also transformed countless hill communities, especially for women who act as labourers and water carriers.

Obviously, my spiel to Atholl wasn't quite this all-encompassing but it was heavy on my passion that these old men in the Himalayas are the most faithful allies we've ever had, and not only is this a debt of honour, but we are in a position to do something about it. The situation is not one of those scary incomprehensible disaster scenarios. 'The £5 per week pension may not sound much, but it can be the difference between survival and utter destitution. I added: 'Scots are very quick and generous to repay this debt,' remembering to flatter donors.

Right on cue, an elderly gent stopped us on the path and without any preliminaries handed over £10. My message in one.

'Did the Gurkhas volunteer for this?'

'Where've you been? Volunteer in the Army? I just told them that it was a cross-country walk with no guard duties for a week!'

By now we were passing three cairns backing on to the Yair Forest, each about eight feet tall and not the usual untidy heap but the locked-tight work of an expert dry stonemason. Known as the Three Brethren, they stand exposed but immovable, each within the properties of Selkirk Burgh, Yair and Bowhill. Photos were taken but the tugging wind nipped like corgis, irritating and spiteful. We were faced with one of life's ironies. At last we had time to take it easy but didn't, for once, have the conditions. The view was dominated by the soaring volcanic plug of the Eildons, culminating in three peaks which the Romans called Trimontium, standing above the Tweed valley. The Moorfoots still lined the north but the purple Lammermuirs lay to the east – the last big feature of the Way.

The elements, though, discouraged a leisurely lunch break. We threw ourselves down on thick grass but the moorland was poor protection from a breeze whose temperature dropped as if in disapproval. Hot coffee and sandwiches were gobbled with unusual gusto. I had mentioned to Atholl that Bishwa's wife was expecting and wondered if it wouldn't be a good story. What I wasn't expecting was that Atholl immediately lent Bishwa his mobile. I know from experience how dangerous can be a Gurkha in possession of a fully functional phone of any kind. It was only a surprise that Bishwa's phone conversation was limited to just ten minutes.

Dhal voiced concern for the escalating toll charge. He nudged Bishwa, but the boy was deaf, bent over the instrument with a concentration that probably only comes when communing with a pregnant wife on another continent.

'The phone call cost £20,' announced Kali cheerfully and emphati-

Overleaf. ***Left:*** **Near Galashiels. Gyan and the boys put on rain jackets as the wind rises.** ***Right:*** **Bishwa's infamous phone call to Nepal. Anguished phone owner sits in background, frowning.**

cally as Bishwa handed the phone back, to winces from us others. Atholl shrugged politely and mumbled something about treating it as a donation. His good manners were clearly hiding a sense of outrage. I'm certain most of us would have expressed some sort of surprise. To top matters, Bishwa's wife had not yet given birth and although Atholl led his eventual piece with the story, there was no culmination. Weeks later he was able to assure me that the toll had not exceeded £10, but that was in the future and for the time being, apologies only were on the agenda.

The wind's malevolence chased and chided us down towards Galashiels, through the Yair Forest until we came to the Tweed, edged by tall beeches with elegantly smooth grey torsos. We crossed the ancient Yair Bridge, a three-span stone construction so old no one knows when it was first built (although there was an act of authorisation to build it in 1764). It is still in heavy use, albeit single traffic only and with an eleven-ton weight limit.

Two girls greeted us who, they announced proudly, had visited Nepal the year before. Kali kind of blew this too. One of them shrugged and told us how her visit had been blighted when struck down by a malady with an exotic Nepali name, 'Jhada'. 'Ah, yes,' said Kali, nodding thoughtfully: 'Diarrhoea.'

'No,' snapped the girl, repeating the illness' name with hurt emphasis.

'Yes, this is Nepali word for diarrhoea,' explained Kali, face beaming and innocent to the rising embarrassment and giggles.

A press photographer took our picture beside a Southern Upland Way sign with what appeared to be a disposable camera. I'm always staggered by what passes as professional photographic equipment on weekly newspapers. Once an Australian girl on *The Oban Star* produced a wee camera from her pocket to snap a large group of old soldiers. I nearly burst out laughing, but at least she had the decency to look embarrassed. However, the Yair Bridge cutting showed us happy with me standing like a schoolteacher beside his charges. The camera always lies. Atholl took a snap with my camera – cutting off our feet – and my face shows unmis-

Opposite: **Yair Bridge. The team is still bursting with energy while I'm trying to look cheerful.**

takable signs of fatigue which surprised me further.

The countryside grew more comfortable, arable with a lush grass we had not seen since the first day. This was obviously fertile farming country. Kali chose the moment to ask if he and Bishwa could stay an extra day with me and leave for Sandhurst, not on the Monday, but Tuesday, while, perhaps, Neil Sahib, 'taking in the Edinburgh Military Tattoo'. Anyone would think the notion had just crossed his mind. 'Yes, of course, but you'll need permission.'

'We already have it! Dhanyabad.[Thanks] Neil Sahib. Can you get tickets now?' Snookered!

Dhal voiced an interest in doing the same and started dialling his HQ in Warwickshire. Only slightly taken aback, but happy, I phoned my colleague, Leigh, back in my Edinburgh office to get me the number of the Tattoo's box office. Within seconds, using my Switch card, we had front row seats for Monday night.

'Is there any special discount for ordering tickets from the most unusual circumstances?' I asked. 'As we speak I'm walking the Southern Upland Way with a group of serving Gurkhas!' There was a giggle at the other end, but no price reductions.

I took a close-up of Bishwa in his rain jacket. It proved to be a smashing photo, perfectly in focus and with a brooding light that captured his taciturn, thoughtful nature like a true portrait. 'That's a good photo,' he said proudly as we both later studied the print. 'Thank you,' he added quietly, entirely missing the point that its excellence was completely due to my outstanding skill and not his talents as a male model. We artists, eh, how easily we're taken for granted.

A close-up of Kali with, what we photographers, but not soldiers, call 'a head shot' ended differently. You know simply from looking through the viewfinder when a good picture presents itself, and Kali's smile, teeth brilliantly white, was a terrific subject. The big portrait lens had only his nearest eye in focus (I admit it, the camera's IQ was way above mine) but just as the shutter opened, Kali turned, giggling and blurring the whole thing. The picture was a write off. Strangely, the same had happened to me a month before – with my three-year-old nephew.

After a couple of hours we were entering Galashiels itself where the girl Kali had accidentally offended re-appeared with her sister and family to invite us for tea in their comfortable house. Hot tea, yes! But what about our dirty boots? Like good country folk, hospitality came before the odd spot of mud. They were the Brydons, whose father had owned the Brydon Creamery and who presented us each with one of his third-of-a-pint bottles as souvenirs. Their generosity exceeded even the norm. We could have stayed for supper. Dhal's improvised walking stick was replaced with a fine hazel thumb stick and we all headed on into the town proper with full bellies too.

The Legion Club on a late Friday afternoon was full of cheerful, smoking drinkers who welcomed us in and sat us down behind pints of lager. There were a lot of those gentle silent smiles and nods which you give wee kids or visiting friends who might not speak English. Mute but warm, it was a common gesture typical of the goodwill the Reivers met everywhere. Only twenty miles or so, it would have been a good idea to pull on tracksuit bottoms over stiffening legs as all we wanted was to be under a hot shower but our kit was in the van. In a nearby pedestrianised street Keith and Campbell were packing up the sales table as it had been agreed we'd find the Club and wait for Campbell to meet us with the van before being dropped at the hotel. The Club was a big affair, on several storeys, giving the overall effect of a layer cake of pubs, each heavy on formica and utilitarian furniture.

It was a proper hotel, with pristine en suite bedrooms and – that hallmark of class – anonymous staff, and all paid for by our wonderful friends at the Legion. Yet again, though, nobody could stop the clock.

The following morning was the Lauder Common Riding, an annual event when four hundred horsemen trot and gallop round the burgh's borders. The streets would be thronged, teeming with excited children and drunken adults, celebrating their heritage in that special Scottish way, including much hard drink. Even teetotallers seem to succumb for the day. Scottish country dancing includes 'reels', a name not chosen by accident. The ceremony is shared by Border towns as far west as Sanquhar (as we had already discovered) though at different times and is always colourful with corporation flags paraded as if they were somehow the 7th Cavalry. Not surprisingly, the event draws big crowds. Custer might be there.

'Neil Sahib, we must wait for table. No problem!' smiled Kali as Dhal and Gyan ordered drinks in the hotel's bar. The restaurant was mobbed with fat-faced blokes in Pringle jerseys stretched over colourful bellies, like spinnakers. Bishwa, a non-drinker, swithered as always between orange juice and tea. Kali, allergic to alcohol, had spent most of his social life sipping tea alongside beer-drinking pals and took it as normal, assuring me that 'If I drink, big red patches come on my body.' The Gurkhali word *raksi* literally means 'rum' but has come to mean 'booze'. This was one of the first things I had learned while acquiring the language and it tells me something about their order of priorities. What my men needed now though was, not bevvy, but food, and preferably a big curry because I knew how unsatisfactory they found our grub, how they played around with it and cleaned the plates only through hunger.

After an hour we were shown a table. The menu was the usual Brit-fare of steak or surf n' turf with oven chips. (Turf? How did *turf* become part of the menu? Turf is a sod of earth with grass attached – doesn't anyone check out these things or is it all left to me?). No rice-based dishes though. There was the usual Brit-salad; wet lettuce and sliced tomato that no one else in Europe would classify as salad exactly; they'd call it wet lettuce and sliced tomato. Ho hum. I used to rave that Brits didn't know any better because they hadn't been abroad. (What do they know of England that only England knows?) but nowadays few haven't. The flaw in all this is that when folk go overseas they eat anglicised food; paella and chips, curries unknown to the subcontinent, and Chinese from a province yet to be discovered, and no garlic for God's sake, 'We're not foreign.' The British actually eat tinned ravioli. I know, I know.

Keith had invited his wife, Alison, to join us, a bigwig in the Red Cross. Kali was fascinated and immediately began probing, in light of her medical knowledge, as to which side she stood on in the great blister debate. The lady had no idea what she was getting into, as we all sat there with tense smiles. She said something about the wisdom of not bursting the thing and protecting it with a plaster. Big mistake. Gyan's eyes grew wide as Kali replied, pointing his knife in emphasis. 'As combat soldier … ' he began, and proceeded to dismantle the lady's expertise with a lack of diplomacy not seen since a sub-editor told Germaine Greer not to both-

Opposite: **Gyan, the steady, complete Gurkha, surveys the scene.**

er her pretty little head. He as good as said she had no idea, really, not compared to an expert like him. We rolled our eyes, but Keith was shaking with laughter as Alison's expression grew more astonished. It's not often a director of the Red Cross has her expertise trashed, discarded, contradicted and trampled upon in public but tonight was the night.

The meal was interrupted by a Legion phone call wanting to know where we were, why we were late, and to let us know that people who had come to see us were already going home. The anguish of obligation known to all fundraisers gripped my heart, setting the pulse thumping. We had no time for a sweet and were already due an apology – all this before we had even arrived. If I was to maintain a humble facade, the augurs were bad. Having worked in an atmosphere of continuous good humour for a week, it was time for a touch of grouchiness. Dhal and Gyan knew the importance of public relations as well as I did but, late and sweetless, there was no pleasure in our steps round to the Club where we knew a scolding awaited.

Our arrival at the Legion Club was officious, even if everyone seemed the worse for drink. A disco on the first floor was halted for our benefit and I gave a brief speech, followed by Gyan in fine form. The good folk of Gala had raised a wonderful £880 by a series of collections within the Club, not from Club funds but from the individual members. This was heartening stuff. The office bearer, mike in hand, standing in the gloom beneath the glitterball, apologised for his drunkenness but explained, perhaps humorously, that he was an alcoholic. The response was silence.

One old soldier in his cups, took my arm to ask stutteringly how to spell 'Gurkha' before more or less dragging his pen across a cheque in slow motion, complete with pauses for deep breaths, sighs and gulps as if this were mentally and physically exhausting. It would have made a humorous cameo in any movie, but left us £20 richer for which 'much thanks'.

'Youse Gurkha bastards,' dribbled a wee man with forceful tone, who tottered over to speak to us, holding his beer before him. 'Ah was in ra Cameronians. Ken wir tartan?' he added aggressively.

'Yes,' I replied uncertainly. 'Douglas.'

'Aye and now youse Gurkha bastards are wearin' it.'

'The Brigade Pipes and Drums,' said Gyan primly. 'I am Queens Gurkha Signals and we wear Grant. The Royal Gurkha Rifles wear Hunting Stewart.'

There was a moment of blind confusion from our man, his crumpled face taking on a new animation as its lines flexed and deepened. You know the type, when he purses his lips they fold inwards. 'See when ah wuz in ra Cameronians – only a few weeks' training in, then intae the Malaya jungle on patrol with youse bastards. Never knew whit hit me. Gurkhas brought back a sack o'communist heads and showed it tae me, laughing. And the risks youse took. Couldnae bluidy believe it. It's alright fer youse to lose your life, but youse were ready to lose mine tae. Only a few weeks I'd been in the army. Youse bastards traumatised me, shouldnae be allowed, ah never forgot it.'

The slurred invective continued for too long, as we fled first to the ground floor only to have him tail us. I was a particular target, obviously an officer, and 'didnae dae anything aboot ra traumas' he'd suffered, 'Youse bluidy Gurkhas.' My anger grew along with the group's bewilderment. Where were the Legion office bearers who should have been quietly taking him aside and at least protecting their guests? This was a club; he was a club member. Wasn't this unacceptable, even shaming behaviour? But nobody came. Gyan looked troubled but continued round the rooms, shaking hands and thanking everyone for their donations.

We left, striding into the warm Friday night, with mixed feelings. Unready to judge the town by the behaviour of one individual, we all knew that not a single person had so much as raised a voice to stop the drunk harassing us. Were they hoping Bishwa would suddenly snap and cut his throat? There is every reason to believe that there was once a local teenager that was unprepared for jungle warfare alongside the wee men from Nepal. There is every reason to suspect that four young Gurkhas will never forget him either. Galashiels, though, had done us proud and our abiding memory was of rising happiness as the trip approached its climax with yet more cash in the bank. We had reived the reivers.

VIII

Galashiels to Longformacus

~~~

The leaving of Gala was not propitious. This was a big day, forty-five kilometres or twenty-seven miles, and it was important that we be on our way by at least our usual 7.30. Hence the rising anguish as, wolfing down bacon and eggs, I noticed the clock was already at 8 a.m. The hung-over chef, forty minutes late for work, had not yet begun making our sandwiches. Deciding that a physical presence might encourage, Gyan and I stood over him in the kitchen. You never saw such an early morning sweat!

But the clearing of Gala itself took us far longer than anticipated and, concerned, I flagged down one of those masters of local geography, a postman, to confirm our location. As always, determined walking took us steadily away from trouble, through the suburbs, past the rugby pitch and down, at last, to the Tweed, with the sun on our faces.

The river looked magnificent, flowing strong and blue in the bright light just like a proper picture-book river. One of the country's great sights, it was superbly uplifting and yet another majestic landmark.

The route was across surprisingly muddy fields but around immense single beeches where cows stood silently as if pondering what to do today. The five passing men in red shirts only served, irritatingly, to distract them momentarily. Nearby stood the stone-faced home of Sir Walter Scott, Abbotsford. It was he who, apart from writing some of the best Border stories of all time, had planted the beech trees.

I was further reminded that, while the Scottish battalions and the Gurkha Rifles have long established regimental links, it was largely men from this area who had officered the Nepalese in the days of their inception. Sir Walter Scott had noted that Indian service had become 'the corn chest for Scotland where we poor gentry must send our youngest sons as we send our black cattle to the South.' The jigsaw pieces were today fitting neatly, not just of my tale, but of history itself. Of course, early morn-
~~~

ing rambles always got me just this side of self-delusion and just that side of self-aggrandisement.

While Gyan's step didn't look entirely comfortable (Dhal and Kali were already seemingly hanging back with him), I was also concerned about a rendezvous with a group of Legionnaires from Melrose who were waiting about a mile ahead. We were perhaps an hour late but communication was impossible as, we discovered later, our contact had left his mobile phone at home.

When the team arrived at the RV the welcoming committee was nowhere to be seen. A flicker of disappointment and guilt flashed through me. We should have met on an old footbridge and could not possibly have missed them. They'd given up and gone home and it was all our fault. I cursed the hotel's inefficiency for being thrown into that dark category of blame with an anger borne of frustration.

'No problem, Neil Sahib. It's not your fault,' said Dhal cheerfully. 'They will send on the cheque. It's just one of those things – at least they weren't waiting in the rain.' Perhaps I take these things too seriously. All the same, it fell to me later both to write and phone apologies.

Melrose and Galashiels have an interesting history of antipathy anyway. Both towns take rugby to levels of obsession not normally regarded as acceptable human behaviour. Melrose Rugby Football Club was formed as a splinter from Gala one night in the 19th century when Melrose men broke into Gala's clubhouse to steal the strips, goal posts and minute book. As if this seedbed of enmity wasn't enough, the Melrose men put it about that Galashiels was the last town in Scotland to have a sewage system. Hence the rugby crowd references to 'The Pail Merks' apparently borne on the backside of everyone from Gala. This story brought great joy, if not incredulity, from our lot who were enchanted that there lurked such aggression in the local blood.

'This is reiver country, you know!' I laughed. The traditions of the Border 'moss trooper' plundering and burning his neighbours then galloping off into the night runs strong hereabouts. My mother is a Kerr, one of the great riding families whose history is a long tale of *News of the World* bloodbaths and little honour, no matter how it is recalled in song and legend. The Reiver Monument, of course, stands in wicked Galashiels.

We thumped across a pedestrian chain suspension bridge which bore many glorious Victorian warning notices. No cattle or horses could use it, but up to 300 cwt could be taken across by hand, the penalty being a stark £2 fine or imprisonment for habitual offenders. There was everything except a ceramic plaque I came across in Kintyre nailed to a rural telegraph pole: 'No throwing stones at the telegraph' in which you could nearly hear the dominie's accent, and see the wagging finger.

A group of walkers stopped us in the centre, announcing that they'd been following our progress in *The Scotsman*. 'Where are you off to today?' 'Longformacus!' said Gyan with slow precision, to gasps and laughs. Yet again I wondered if the old bitten-off-too-much-to-chew scenario loomed. Then an empty minivan was encountered, which we'd seen at Traquair, with a self-satisfied driver informing us that her passengers, Edinburgh teachers, were way ahead of us on the route to Lauder.

The lads did what they always did, laughed happily. My discouragement evaporated; we were, as ever, on our own and up for anything. I was fit, in a hurry and my blood was roaring.

In fact, the route showed farmland with only the occasional wandering contour – the whitest map we'd seen – and a long Roman road which should provide no great challenge so long as we could hit a fast stride and keep it.

For an hour the lads kept a cracking pace as our country road was eaten up, its hedges of brambles, elder and beech sprocketed past as in a film. Nowadays, not much more than a Land Rover track, but once it had rung to the tramp of numberless Roman legionnaires. We were now part of that history. My mind, obviously, was beginning to self-stimulate.

Dhal and Gyan had stopped ahead of me, heads looking back. 'Where's Kali and Bishwa?'

I turned round too, groaning. 'Christ, where are the wee bastards?' We waited a minute before Dhal and Gyan continued. I tried phoning the missing duo but both numbers were unaccountably engaged.

The dread began to form as a certainty. 'Oh no, please don't have wandered off,' I said under my breath and started jogging back the way we'd come. In my mind's eye I could already see a lost hour or two looming – and all because I'd dozed off. 'Kali! Bishwa!' I yelled to the echoless horizon, growing certain that they'd taken a wrong turning two miles back but uncertain whether to keep dialling or let them phone me.

My impatient irritated step changed into a thundering lope as the big boots accelerated into a dinosaur lumber and my calls became elephantine trumpeting. A sudden halt would be impossible, or at least very painful but not without comedic possibilities. Eventually, I saw them, to my anger, squatting on the track, neither hurt nor lost but apparently having a chat. I bawled at them. The figures jumped to their feet and ran towards me with Kali shouting 'Sorry, Neil Sahib, sorry!'

We jogged angrily at a fierce lick to Dhal and Gyan. Both Bishwa and Kali had taken it upon themselves, without telling me, to decide this was the ideal time of day to call round a few friends in Nepal and waste about twenty minutes – not forgetting my valuable reserves of energy. I was fizzing, unable to believe they could have done something so thoughtless. In fact, there wasn't a problem with them stopping; they could have caught up in minutes with their deer-like fleetness, but the twosome had put me through a panic by disappearing. 'Don't ever do that again!' I shouted in genuine anger, certain that with barely twenty-four hours to go they wouldn't transgress between now and tomorrow afternoon.

'Did you give them a good bollocking?' asked Dhal hopefully. 'Don't they know we're pressed for time?'

I grunted quietly, which Dhal took to mean it was up to him to have words with the miscreants. The same sentiments were flung back at them, albeit in good Gurkhali, until they were the very picture of penitent school kids. You half expected Bishwa to say, 'Please sir, Kali made me do it.'

The incident was quickly forgotten though and my concern transferred to Gyan whose pace, even with the muscular use of a walking stick, was threatening slow lane stuff. An unpleasant decision was forming.

Dhal and I were fit, while Bishwa and Kali could, if ordered, happily skip all the way to the North Sea and back again, but if Gyan was to continue after lunch his progress could only deteriorate. Furthermore, the prospect of Gyan not participating in tomorrow's finish was unthinkable.

I sidled up. 'Gyan. I have been watching you today, and when we reach Lauder at lunch I want you to stay there and help Keith and Campbell. Understand? You simply must be fit for tomorrow; it's only seventeen miles. I think you ought to rest this afternoon.'

This was very difficult. Gyan was the sort of friend that would come from the ends of the world for my funeral – and I his – but it had to be done. All because of just two blisters but the greater good must be served. This was a tremendous blow to Gyan's pride, and I knew it.

He didn't look up, concentrating on his walking stick but quietly assented. There was no doubt in my mind and Gyan knew too. Our speed, however, never let up, not even for Gyan. It was, literally, a blistering pace. There was, though, a moment when we pulled to one side to allow a teenage girl on a white horse to ride past. Our war cry had been 'Ramro Ketiharu!' (Good Women) and I couldn't helping announcing 'Ramro Keti!' (Good Woman) to a round of guffaws. She was a pretty girl but young, nervous and even when we greeted her in English her uncertainty didn't entirely disappear but gave a tight 'hello', probably unaware that Kali's sigh of appreciation was for the white horse, not her. I wondered who she thought we were and laughed to myself.

The road became a path and suddenly we were descending into Lauder through baby bracken with the heather-clad Lammermuirs on the far side of the valley. There seems to be a region-wide name shortage for rivers in the Borders. If there wasn't the Gala Water at Gala or the Yarrow Water at Yarrow there was the Ettrick Water at, er, Ettrick. The valley ahead was cleaved by the Lauder Water. There has, of course, never been a shortage of yer actual water in the Borders.

Entering the town we passed a couple of horseboxes with two floppy-haired guys in white riding breeches sitting on camp chairs like young princes, surrounded by young women. As we tramped towards this scene of adoration, the girls turned to look.

'Ah, the Gurkhas! We've been ahead of you for two days but always there were those red shirts in the distance, catching up!' greeted one. I was surprised. No one had been on the horizon as far as we knew but these were the Edinburgh teachers whose van we'd passed both at Traquair and this morning.

'We've been reading about you in *The Scotsman*. I think one day it was out of synch!' said another while I agreed that young Simon Pia had settled quite well into his new job as diarist, and was sure he'd go a long way. The teachers were delighted to meet us but true to form, our boys were suddenly mute. The floppy-hairs in the background shifted in their chairs, obviously unhappy if not indignant to have the female attention transferred. It was for moments like this that I'd planned the whole trip.

Alas, we had to push on. Lauder, despite being full of people and not a parking space to be had, showed only deserted streets. The entire population, visiting or resident, was squeezed into the pubs. Finding Keith and Campbell in the main street was easy. Standing behind a market stall selling Gurkha Welfare Trust goods, they were about the only people there, albeit joined by a couple of GWT worthies, including Major Alec Power, a man known to us all.

Along with my feet, part of my head goes numb with concentrated, robotic, speed-walking. We had covered eighteen miles in just over four hours and it was impossible suddenly to switch channels to another mode. Aware that I was not at my most communicative, I had a quick coffee, explained what was what and led the group out of the town. Gyan, impassively, took a seat in Campbell's support vehicle but I wasn't about to relent. Being so target-orientated seemed to affect my persona and powers of PR, but our trip was dominated by two factors: time and distance. Our achievements were dependant not on one, but both, and we must keep going. It was just after 1 p.m.

Somewhere on the outskirts Kali began to rant with that frantic petulance we knew from the blisters row: 'You have been unfair to Gyan. Is not right. We are together. Is unfair. Is not right.'

'Kali!' I countered. 'Gyan is not fit. It is better he is fit for tomorrow.' Dhal added some soothing words and the squall blew over. The next problem was tackling the Lammermuirs which I realised, with growing wonder, was nowhere near the agony I had expected. Looking at my knees, I marvelled at their new-found strength. Climbing had not just become easier but downright comfortable. The upward slopes were, to my knees, friends not enemies. They drove uphill like well-tuned engines, albeit lower end of the market Trabant engines compared with the premium machines of my pals. Alec Power had told me of how he'd tried to keep up with his Gurkha platoon as they raced up the scree of a North West Frontier hillside just after the War. It was quite impossible but, as he toiled upwards, he could be confident of staying in touch on the way down. Wrong. Gurkhas bound down scree like high-speed mountain

Overleaf. ***Left:*** **Dhal and Kali enjoy a quick break. Stops became briefer as the march neared its end.** ***Right:*** **Approaching Lauder with the Lammermuirs behind, our last major obstacle.**

GURKHA REIVER

goats, and left him on the skyline panting his heart out.

A neatly trimmed field set on a slope was the first proper rest of the day. The route seemed to cross about a hundred grid squares on the map before meeting our destination but it was straight and uncomplicated. The weather was calm and dry underfoot. Conditions couldn't have been better. The boys sat crunching crisps, Kali, with several crow feathers poking from his cap and happily asking for confirmation as to how well we were doing.

'We're on course, Kali, but as always we're short of time,' I said before adding: 'Time hath, my lord, a wallet at his back wherein he puts alms for oblivion.'

'For oblivion,' nodded Kali knowingly, to snorts from Dhal and Bishwa.

I was silently kicking myself for not having covered extra miles the day before but was aware that it was too late for regrets. I was in no condition to kick anyone anyway, least of all myself. We had enjoyed an easy stroll yesterday, too easy, and this afternoon we'd break the last back of the whole walk. However, an unspoken confidence had always imbued the team but now it began to bloom.

The road was a stony track through a broad heather moor, the horizons low and level on all sides, our movement marked only by the slow passing of forestry plantations far to our right and left. Since the top of Lowther Hill our pace had become steadily unremitting. Miles were there to be knocked off the clock.

A fat adder moved, writhing into the verge, the first I'd seen for years, its zigzag back unmistakable. 'Look!' I pointed. Within a second Dhal was upon it, hazel raised, whooping.

'No!' I shouted, but too late as the snake lay brainless, its sticky blood like crimson syrup. 'Are adders endangered or protected species?' I wondered, panicking. The phrase 'writhed snake-like' is, I realised, inadequate to describe the whirling, hitching motion. They don't writhe at all – especially when missing their heads. We were to see many but Dhal left them alone.

In quite a different category were rabbits and hares which Dhal and Bishwa appeared to locate by internal radar. Again and again the duo would leap into the heather, Dhal covering the left, Bishwa the right, to frighten the life out of some furry creature that would bolt off only to crouch up ahead in what it thought was safety, unaware that its position was marked on a mental chart. Grouse would rise in formation and skim the hillside like fighter-bombers, looking for a landing spot too distant for our attention.

'I used to work on a grouse-beating estate up north,' I said.

'How did you kill them?' asked Dhal, as if I could, today perhaps, help out.

'Well, I didn't, but the others used shotguns.'

'Shotguns?' his voice betraying shock as if this wasn't quite fair against such large slow targets.

'Yes, and the shooting season begins next Saturday. The Glorious Twelfth. This is as big as the grouse population gets.'

Two immense cairns, the Twin Laws, had stood on the skyline for hours like some portals from Conan the Barbarian and were only 500 metres inside Berwickshire. Even these were now behind us and the plateau fell away to another but the view was full of quilted fields, copses, farmhouses and even a small reservoir, the Watch Water, its surface blue under the August sun. I had hoped to glimpse a triangle of the North Sea from here but it was beyond the horizon. Tomorrow though.

Gyan and Campbell were waiting in the van like two solicitous wally dugs set behind the dashboard. If there was ever a more attentive support worker than Campbell, I've yet to meet one. It was always he who had to do the shopping and run about fulfilling small requests. He was the only one of us who seemed to be permanently happy to be here every single minute of the day. Gyan seemed content and rested, which was a relief as I dreaded a sulk, but these guys seemed strangers to huffs. Longformacus is a perfect hamlet with stone cottages clad in roses. A note hung from the bus stop. 'Dear Gurkhas, Please call at the house opposite.'

Intrigued, we did just that, my knees numb and slowly locking. A cheery healthy man emerged with those tiny ears, close to the skull, that look like they've been in a deep fat fryer and then ironed flat. He had collected £60 for us, from the Post Office, I think, and presented the sum in

Overleaf. ***Left:*** **Dhal with thumbstick he had mysteriously acquired in Galashiels. He said it was a gift.** ***Right:*** **Gyan leads Bishwa and Kali in early morning sun.**

small change. It was typical of small town Scotland and no less sweet for that.

'Neil, there are two girls in this B&B,' said Gyan, pointing, 'who want to see us too. They made a £20 donation.'

'What do they look like?' asked Dhal quickly.

'Okay,' answered Gyan, offhand.

The girls were either in the bath or just out, but they came cheerfully on to the road in dressing gowns, drying their hair. They were English and had read about us in the press. There was no family link, no father or grandfather who had fought in Burma; they just wanted to make a donation and meet the boys. Walkers too, they had taken two weeks to cover the 195 miles to this spot that had taken us eight days. There was a relief map of the Way set in stone outside the B&B which we all fingered like inquisitive children. Gyan presented two Gurkha tea towels which were received like sacred relics. Oh, our boys could make friends all right, and money, loads of money.

The minibus took us to another ancient Border town, Jedburgh, where we were put in a comfortable B&B. Even the en suite bathrooms could have been from the Hilton. Scotland does not have the best reputation in the world for good B&Bs and the Tourist Board sells itself a wee bit like this was Nepal: wonderful scenery but don't expect comfort. Someone should write a guidebook to the astounding taste of Scotland's more adventurous landladies. In one B&B, I recall, amid all the usual paraphernalia from the barrows of Torremolinos, was a collection of bas-relief plates hanging on the wall, each depicting a European capital. The Eiffel Tower, an Amsterdam bridge and the Brandenberg Gate stood in spray paint, garishly bright, as if spattered with sherbet. Our hostess couldn't but help notice my bulging eyes. 'Got them all in Malaga!' she enthused: '£20 the lot!' 'Really?' I gasped, in genuine surprise. 'That much?' The next room had an entire wall exhibiting hundreds of cheap china animals that I was ushered round to see in hushed reverence. In an Inverness hall stood a six-foot high glass case holding a four-foot Princess Diana doll in a sequinned high-collared white dress. I couldn't help but stare at the thing as our hostess wrung her hands in proud delight. I think part of my brain died that afternoon.

Gyan and I had little time to enjoy the comfort of our room as, within minutes, we were showered, changed and tucking into a pasta supper in the Legion clubrooms. This one was run by both the Regimental Secretary of the King's Own Scottish Borderers, Colonel Colin Hogg, and the former managing director of Exacta Circuits, George Millar, and, boy, did it show. The supper was ideal, and not entirely foreign to the lads. It could be smothered in chilli sauce or eaten with fresh *khorsani* and, as every athlete knows, pasta loads you up with calories. If pork were a Nepalese dish, which it isn't, you could have said we were in hog heaven.

There was just a small friendly group of about twelve gathered round the table, with conversation relaxed and chatty. I was called upon to recount my funny Gurkha story. There was once a brand new Gurkha officer, a *saunu sahib*, inspecting his first guard as orderly officer outside the guardroom. He was determined to pick up at least one soldier for something but discovered they were all immaculately turned out. Frustrated but resolved to catch out someone, he asked one soldier: 'You! What would you do tonight if you saw someone crawling towards your position from those bushes over there?' 'Ah, Sahib,' replied the young rifleman: 'I'd carry him back to the officers' mess.'

The tale nicely encapsulates the Gurkhas' attitude towards their British officers: humorous, respectful but slightly condescending. There is always that unique Gurkha look which twinkles: 'You are very lucky, you know, to have me as your soldier.' I, of course, laughed my head off at my own joke as if I were Billy Connolly. We were feeling good.

Later was time for relaxed lagers with Dhal, as usual, standing at the bar in dark blazer, white shirt and tie, chatting up the barmaid, Gyan making his public relations round of handshakes, Kali fascinated with something he'd discovered (like a Swiss army knife), and Bishwa quiet but taking everything in (just what would his diary say about us?). All four stood in their usual enormous brogues, known delightfully as 'Shoes Highland' which gave them great big cartoon-like feet and made loss of balance impossible. Jedburgh was everything we wanted: happy, generous and welcoming. And no sign of a drunken ex-Serviceman, pawing our shoulders and demanding attention. No wonder Mary Queen of Scots visited –

Overleaf. ***Left:*** **Where the heck are we? Answer: somewhere east of Portpatrick.** ***Right:*** **Dhal with feathered friend taken into temporary custody.**

GURKHA REIVER

the town that is – not the British Legion.

It was midnight when we walked up the main street to our B&B but were stopped by two cops investigating a smashed shop window, its two-tone alarm whining and light flashing. 'Good grief!' said one cop, 'Gurkhas! Well, it obviously wasn't you! On your way now. Take care and good luck!' And that was the message from the community too.

IX

Longformacus to Cockburnspath

~~~

Stretching out the map in the middle of the road at Longformacus, the early sunlight pierced through the elm leaves to strike my forearms. The skin was nearly as brown as that of my colleagues, who were fingering the final day's route, a red line meandering to the right edge of my very last map.

It was only seven o'clock and we were promised a dazzling day. Fit and ready, we stood up, kicked a few stones and strolled, really strolled, up a silent lane lined with beeches, their grey trunks shining like the legs of newly scrubbed elephants. Five-and-a-half hours sleep was all that we had allowed ourselves, the deep dreamless stuff of high health and round contentment. Well, at least it was for me. Gyan complained that I was a *bahg*, a tiger, meaning that I snored (the noise is supposed to be similar to the big cat's growl). At last, I'm a tiger in bed, but in the wrong language and with quite the wrong meaning.

I had wanted the guys up at 5.30 and to get the last stage over pronto, a sentiment accepted readily. There had been the usual gargantuan breakfast of fruit, Weetabix, plug-your-arteries fry up, followed by rounds of toast and marmalade. It seemed impossible to over-eat at this time of day, although learning early on that coffee noticeably dehydrated me, I gulped down at least one pot of tea instead. We were understandably grateful that the B&B's proprietors had gone along with our early start. Gyan presented them with a Gurkha teddy bear – a gift that was always greeted with huge smiles and certainly did the trick for us this time.

In the area's long history, there can't have been many more happy to have been in Berwickshire. Progress was light-hearted albeit with that dogged determination which had underscored our every step since

Overleaf. ***Left:*** **The lads laughing and confident while I am happy but bewildered.** ***Right:*** **Abbey St. Bathans. The bridge that Kali reckoned required his engineering skills.**
~~~

Portpatrick. Gyan was stoic though, wearing an expression normally associated with biting too-tough toffee. He had at last stopped chaffing about an extra set of maps but, judging by his frown, was berating the patron saint of quality footwear. Bishwa was, like yesterday, wearing only light trainers, while Kali, as always, was clad in tracksuit bottoms as if there was never going to be a day that really pushed him. Dhal, ever ready to perform drum major antics with his thumb stick, ambled happily. For myself, my knees had surpassed themselves, princes among patellas. The combined age of my knees was eighty-six, for God's sake, their joint age you might say. How had my body been able to accomplish all this without breaking down? Was it muscle memory, will power or genuine fitness? I looked round at our bunch. No silly health foods among them, not even a grain bar, no trekking poles and not a multi-coloured jacket in sight. My God, we were practically unique. I couldn't see Kali in rainbow Gore-Tex anyway. Red polo-shirts and thin green cagoules are not likely to be taken up by the shiny outdoor set in their magentas and day-glo multi-terrain 'systems'. In design terms, our kit may have been primitive but it worked and I wouldn't have swapped it for the entire catalogue of the fancy stuff sold by all the outdoor 'pursuits' shops in all of Scotland.

An invigorating breeze ruffled the long grass and gorse as we tramped towards the final goal under a perfect blue sky and brilliant sunlight, surrounded by dazzling colours and the blackest of shadows.

It was still early Sunday morning, as curtained country houses reminded us, but striding up a small rise, Dhal was as sharp as ever. As if to prove the point he'd occasionally stoop to snatch a young pheasant from the undergrowth. The technique was to swing the hazel like a squash racquet dropshot, stunning the bird with a body blow, then grab it by the legs – all in a smooth second. It must be said that the birds somehow didn't look unhappy, mildly surprised perhaps but uncomplaining, as if only hearing that they hadn't won the lottery that weekend. Dhal would give the bird a quick kiss and release it. An act of surprising grace, it exhibited a paradox; if he had such affection for the bird why was he part-braining them so happily.

'Could we take these home, Neil Sahib?' asked the inevitable Kali.

Instinctively, I knew there was no one like my Gurkha lads. We were the sunny mile-eaters, free of everything, crunching our way to the eastern seaboard of Scotland with certain tread and assured, unspoken, self-confidence. We were the Gurkha Reivers, united and beating everything that trends, doubters and fate could throw at us. In context, we were just five people about to finish a not very famous walk but were happy for all that. I knew that I could never have done this without them, their merry company and earnest encouragement. There was always that extra pull on my will power brought about simply by being with them. I was keeping up with the Gurkhas, and, wow, wasn't it exhilarating?

By early afternoon and twenty-eight kilometres the whole blasted expedition would be complete and we could be entitled to a sense of achievement. Fulfilment of even small dreams is rare but every dog has its day – though I was still fretting about how we were to get back to my flat, bathe and then make the most of a reception at the British Legion Club in Edinburgh. Seems fatalistic, I know, but the past eight days had taught me to foresee disasters, not anticipate coups. Nevertheless, I could sense internally the rising strains of triumphant music (and a touch of melodrama). We were on our way.

Before long we came across the box girder bridge at Abbey St Bathans, famously built by the Queen's Gurkha Engineers and spanning the Whiteadder. Despite a relaxed pace we had covered about a third of the day's target and, with time on our hands, it was an occasion to relax with some cold cans. Unfortunately, there was no abbey to offer succour, nor ever had been: the name is a misnomer, but a lady directed us to a shop and pub which was about half a mile off route. Leaving Gyan stretched out on a bench like a lazy big cat, we jogged down the lane to find this pub. To be off route, and galloping along too, seemed a furious waste of energy, especially in the rising heat. The lane was bordered with high hedges in full summer density which together with the road's curves meant we couldn't even see our destination nor gauge how far we'd come. One thing was certain: our pub or shop was much further than indicated.

So it was with hot frustration that we kicked the pub's dusty car park. We'd over-looked the time, 10.30 a.m., and it was as quiet as an empty hillside. Furthermore, a slim man in his thirties called from the adjacent trout farm to tell us that the shop had closed down. Jesus Christ! Kali, Bishwa and Dhal had marched a mile, and with the whole world to blame, I couldn't fault anyone but myself. Sorry guys.

Deciding we couldn't bear to retrace our steps, the group walked back along the riverbank, whacking wild rhubarb and giant hogweed.

Gyan had actually fallen asleep. As we hunkered down, pouring coffee and tea, he awoke and asked for a can of drink – Diet Coke, if you please. Dhal gruffly informed him of the facts.

A young woman, holding a wash basket of shirts to her hip, stopped to chat. Not only did she fondly remember the Gurkha troop that had built the bridge but could recall the wonderful nightly parties held during its construction. The period had been suspiciously long, a month, I think, implying that our friends in the Engineers, if slow, took public relations very seriously. Her husband had been the guy at the trout farm. We had now walked for two-hundred miles but it seemed mentally not far, almost over there. This woman saw the distance as we did and understood it like us too. The ancient comprehension of land and distance, shanks pony stuff, was curiously alive in her like no one else we met.

We sat in the sun for probably too long, unhurried and self-virtuous with our early start. The coffee and cigarettes were stimulants within the law but sinful for all that.

'C'mon guys, let's take a picture of you on the bridge.' The foursome was photographed with the guys, legs dangling, like a bunch of boy scouts. The image appeared later in a local paper with an imaginative quote from Gyan claiming it would always have a place in his heart. I remember Gyan telling a journalist elsewhere: 'The response of the Scottish people has been 110%,' as if he were in training for football management and that any minute now he'd be over the moon and getting a result on a trip of two halves.

'This bridge, Neil Sahib, not good, too much wood used,' opined Kali. 'I make better bridge. I take your photo now.' The subsequent print proved to be the only one he took that was in focus. I'm sitting with soles towards camera, looking bewildered but surprisingly tanned.

'Let's go!' The Reivers tramped across the road straight into what seemed like a hallucination as a hundred Swedish school children came out of nowhere and barged past. We gawped in amazement. Their chatter

Opposite: **Bishwa leads Kali. I swear these two could have skipped the whole way and back again.**

and nonchalance implied they had no idea as to where they were. They weren't scanning the hillsides; they were looking at each other. A flock of blonde starlings in multi-coloured jackets. They employed the casual urban pace used back in civilisation when going to the shops or the pub. It was totally different to our stride. They had no rhythm. Their teachers nodded silently but we made no eye contact with anyone else. This too was different. On the hill, the least polite act possible was to nod and greet. Blimey, how long had we been away?

The little Whiteadder valley was full of oaks, and they remained on our left for a half-mile as we climbed to, surely, the last plateau. It was about here, at Devenish, that movement became robotic. The anxiety to finish was rising, the wish to dawdle diminishing as the team began to strain as a unit, striding on and on. The ever grander farmhouses and lush pastures passed more and more quickly. There was more than the sun on my back; there was a deep fatigue sitting on my shoulder. Like a marathon runner hitting the wall, my reserves were nearly finished.

A farm track full of egg-sized stones followed the edge of a pine plantation which seemed appallingly long but, if my calculations were correct, there was a farm at the end of it called Blackburn from which I should espy the sea, like stout Cortez and an accompanying group of Nepalese.

We cleared the wood, tramped past the stone-built farmhouse, the pan-tiled barns and a row of 4x4s, and then saw, nestling in the valley's distant cleavage, a triangle of brilliant divine blue – the North Sea, at last. The sight my eyes had yearned for. The precise moment of seeing it for the first time is burned into my memory. Never was a glimpse of blue so glorious.

The moment was as good as any to rest. The roadside was grassy, and lined like a row of arboreal lampposts with a series of horse chestnuts. The paddock behind was fenced with white-washed wooden palings normally associated with horses. But it was hot. 'Oh look!' I opened one of those new-fangled sealed Kit Kats to discover the chocolate was running round inside like warm cocoa. 'What did you expect?' asked Dhal, quietly both impassive and dismissive. I guiltily tossed the whole thing over the fence, catching Gyan's eye, who grinned conspiratorially.

Kali stood up, and with a stick lifted the carcase of a recently dead hedgehog. 'Neil Sahib, this is guinea pig?' 'No, hedgehog.' 'Ah, guinea pig!' The guy was irrepressible.

Impossible to eat, we sipped hot tea and gently smoked. 'Right guys, last stretch!' I said, symbolically with arms wide. Puns, which require a level of understanding of the language, had been off limits for a week, but I still tried. A huge curving country road took us down towards our goal. Kali was in full voice, and most of us were singing along. The map showed another seven or eight miles when a tall lean figure in shorts and dark glasses came lumbering up the hill. It took me a second to recognize him. 'Mero bhai!' My brother!

Ewen came up, shook hands with everyone and almost with embarrassment announced that we could be heard for miles around. His alien white legs made me realise how brown were mine. 'About an hour to go!' he chirruped to cheers, 'and all downhill!' Where had we heard that last bit?

We were quickly across the busy A1, the main east-coast London-Edinburgh route which seemed crazily full of speeding vehicles, and then along and across the main railway line. There were heaps of walkers but we were striding past like champions through the Penmanshield Wood, an appalling series of rises and falls through dog-rose and bracken. Where was *The Scotsman's* Fordyce Maxwell, he of the Private Frazer-like prediction? His diarist colleague, Simon Pia, had joked in print that Fordyce would join us for the last one-hundred yards. Knowing our pace, in the blazing heat, would be too uncomfortable for a Sunday walker, I suddenly hoped the joke would be true. My brother, without a pack and fit, gave no concern though. Fordyce, I heard later, came up with a novel but truthful get out; his daughter was moving house. Without further Farming Editors ado, we thumped on, my temples soaking. Fordyce, Simon and I met up the next day anyway, for a rib-poking, back-slapping session.

Then, at last, below lay the entire North Sea with views to Fife and the cube-like Torness power station in dazzling white to our left. Had our eyes picked out Norway too, it would not have surprised me one jot. It was that kind of moment.

Overleaf. ***Left:*** **The route is well marked; gates were always available. Note Bishwa in trainers as usual.** ***Right:*** **The North Sea at last, but surprises were in store.**

Against the backdrop I'd been waiting for since Portpatrick, we posed for three or four snaps. Uplifted as we were, no one could raise a smile. Each of us is grim-faced with hair plastered with sweat. Only Kali looks elfishly delighted and his hair is wet too, like Bishwa's. The strain was telling. My body, for one, had been pushed to its limits but the compensation was that this was now nearly over. Wrong!

We descended down chickenwire-clad wooden steps to the sea past a group of white caravans reminiscent of Llandudno to then face a series of steep cliff climbs towards the fabled Cockburnspath. At the back of our heads was a jubilation, an exultation, that we had made it to the sea but 80% of the brain was saying, don't celebrate yet, it's not over 'till the fat Reiver sings'. Dichotic achievement or what? The remaining miles were agonizing, easily the toughest we'd done. Concern grew about Gyan whose grim features were set in inadmissible pain. I nudged him to the front with Ewen knowing that from here on in pride was the spur.

At last, after what seemed like a tour round a Blackpool caravan site, we came along the steep cliffs that lead into the tiny village of Cockburnspath. On one side a tremendous drop to its Lilliputian harbour and on the other a barley field, lately harvested.

'Last field!' I said encouragingly. Then, horror, just as we were about to enter the village the signpost pointed the other way. For some bizarre reason, the route designers had decided that arrivals take a two kilometre detour via the railway underpass. The frustration of this double blow: first you reach the sea and then continue for a half hour, climbing up and down, to be followed by an entirely arbitrary detour nearly tempted us into a short cut, forgetting all about the route to the blasted underpass. We weren't by now just mere colleagues and fellow travellers, each was a pilgrim – a *nedrog*, a companion on the path of life.

The hot gravel of that path under my boots remains with me yet. No words of encouragement were needed. This was our day. No matter what some idiotic bastard had decreed, we would do it.

The eventual finish unravelled without further surprises. We re-entered the village, half expecting another detour, and, like a cowboy film, spread into an extended silent line across the main street, our boots crunching in time, marching up to the Mercat Cross in the blazing sun. All that was needed was the clink of spurs. We'd done it.

The reception committee was small but ecstatic. 'So, Neil, I imagine you're very proud of yourself,' smiled my brother. Fatigue swept over me like a numb wave. I couldn't answer. Gathering the guys together, we shook hands exchanging *shyabashes* and *thulo shyabashes* (well done and very well done) with an intensity that comes from near exhaustion and close friendship. We had crossed farmland, heaths, mountains and moorland, broad-leafed and coniferous woodlands, edged past lochs, rivers, reservoirs, sea cliffs and shores. We had stridden through villages and towns. We had done the Southern Upland Way.

Alec Power, friend and former Gurkha officer, provided champagne which I knew my body didn't want, but after three hot cups of tea the bubbly was irresistible. The local community council, bless 'em, had laid on sandwiches and buttered fruit cake which no one could face but their head, an intelligent woman in her sixties, pushed a cheque on me. There were some guys from the Bridge of Weir British Legion Club who, irritatingly, demanded a video interview but, later, I was very glad to receive the cassette as a souvenir.

We sat on the burning steps of the Mercat Cross in floods of sunshine for photos. One was to be reproduced in magazines many times. In one, I looked younger than I had for years. That was the one sent to Joanna Lumley, of course.

With hindsight I can see that this was a defining moment. I should have been the happiest man in Scotland. A life moment, except that I was far too tired. Ewen's comment was almost unacknowledged, and slung like so many other compliments into the sinking mire of exhaustion.

The video man from Bridge of Weir insisted on a wee song which our boys supplied like old hands: We were the trooper troupers. It was the jam, jam, jama jam from Newcastleton which I knew and joined in, clapping cheerfully – *jam* means blink. From the tape you would never know how utterly weary we were.

The van's sliding door crashed shut and we headed back to my flat in Edinburgh. While parts of my body were on fire, the rest was numb, including the synapses. After two minutes I turned round from the front passenger seat to say something very important, as usual. Everyone was fast asleep. Dhal lolled immobile like a casualty while Kali and Bishwa slept in each other's arms, a common and touching Gurkha habit. It was only 2.30 p.m. While they were dreaming, I seemed to be in a dream.

The flat seemed strangely clean. Discarding my now grey boots (they had been blue) and able to savour thick carpeting beneath my toes, it became obvious that I would be the source of much undignified humour on a forthcoming Greek holiday. While my legs were brown, the feet were milk white. What was I going to do? Spend the first few days with my feet stuck out of the window?

At 6.30 p.m. on the dot we entered the Royal British Legion Scotland Club, the Edinburgh Central Branch, where the group met up with Keith, and my colleague Leigh, for the last formal function of our trip. A full crowd of the white cardie brigade filled the hall, bobbing heads reminiscent of a breeze moving through a cotton field. A handsome cheque for £2,000 was presented and the draw made for the raffle where, no matter what we did, almost every prize was won by someone from Newcastleton. My speech of thanks was nearly my best but marred by a sweat that simply wouldn't stop. Perhaps it was an over-reaction to the heat or exhaustion, but Kali came running with a pink paper napkin which was almost as embarrassing as the sweat itself. Imagine a bloke under a shower with a microphone and you'll have the picture.

Later a woman asked: 'Are you a Gurkha?'

'No,' I replied, 'But I've been with Gurkhas for the past week!'

'Are you sure you're not a bit Gurkha? You look dark enough.'

'No, I'm quite sure that I'm not a Gurkha, but I've been asked before if I'm foreign.'

'That's it. You look foreign,' as if a great truth had been revealed, then adding the inarguable: 'You're too tall for a Gurkha.'

At this point a dolled-up couple in their late sixties took the floor and, astonishingly, began belting out 'My Bonnie Lies Over the Ocean'. They were truly terrible with him howling like a drunk (which he may have been) while she vibratoed like a comic opera diva, waving her arms around like Hattie Jacques swotting flies. The audacity was remarkable; you weren't sure whether this was a comedy turn but whatever, it certainly garnered wild applause. It was at this point that the Master of Ceremonies, probably spotting my shoulders heaving in laughter or the tears rolling down my cheeks, pointedly asked me, by name, 'to remove yourself' from the bar, if I wasn't buying anything. 'House rules, Mr

Griffiths!' The hall turned to tut.

Slightly ashamed but enraged too, I retreated to inspect a notice which read: 'Members are not permitted to reserve seats for patrons not deemed on the premises.' This was not a legal debate in which the word 'deemed' could be scrutinised and probed. It said, dinnae even think aboot bagging seats for pals that arnae here. Walls plastered with facetious notices were a feature of every Legion club. The invention of the laser printer has a lot to answer for. While 'Swearing is prohibited at all times' gives an inkling as to the usual patron and how management chose to respond to its wickedness, it always raised a laugh to read: 'Can You Prove Your Age?' We're the boys that have seen the Walking Stick Tango, almost literally the Last Waltz, and had rarely come across anyone aged under forty. Toilets, too, were, apparently, information centres with instructions as to washing hands and directives concerning where urine should be deposited with handy reminders such as: 'We aim to please, you aim too, please'. No bar was without the 'You don't have to be mad to work here but the impossible takes longer' stuff. The days of the Gestetner are well and truly gone. Alas, among the many cautions I had missed the one about no loitering at the bar or you'll be ritually humiliated by the bloke with the mike. However, if someone gives a cheque for £2,000 every time they insult me, they can gladly have all night. The good folk of the British Legion were beyond that, and again I experienced a genuine emotion of gratitude for their repeated generosity.

We parted to a nearby bar where an Asian business man eaves-dropped. Overhearing my Gurkhali, he burst out laughing. When I cast an enquiring eye he explained: 'You Nepalese! You can't pronounce your Ss!' For a second I was startled, then as happy as hearing that smoking was good for you. He thought I was a Gurkha! Toying with the idea of pushing my hair back and in best Fettes voice declaring: 'My dear chap ...' I settled for a delighted laugh. His name, it transpired, was Dennis. 'Dennis?' I repeated, grinning. Good grief, I thought, I *am* in the wrong movie.

Later, much later, we sat around my diningroom table. Clad only in

Overleaf: *Left:* **Not far now. Dhal walks the walk past Abbey St Bathans.** *Right:* **The end is near as Gyan, left, begins to make muscular use of his stick to alleviate blisters.**

shorts, we at last ate together, untrammelled by convention, unrestricted by demands but simply as good friends. There were bottles of coke, mineral water and wine before us, heaps of fried and boiled rice, curry galore, every type of small finger delicacy, prawn crackers, mini spring rolls, and dishes of deeply-coloured dips. There had been no meal like it. The lads ate mostly with their hands. I hadn't experienced such an atmosphere since schoolboy ends of term. This was the defining moment for the Gurkha Reivers: triumphant, united and happy.

My friends, I thought, brought up in the thin icy air beneath the eternal snows on small farms high in the greatest mountains on the planet, had been everything I'd ever heard. Their shoeless childhoods, labouring in an environment too punishing for all but they, had produced men of indomitable physique and spirit. *Ma jasto kohli chhaina*, they say simply: there is no one like me. I know that now, it rings true like a perfectly cast bell. The poem *To a Gurkha* contains a profound truth:

When God first chose a Gurkha
As a vessel of His own,
He took a chunk of cheerfulness
And laid on flesh and bone,
A face, well some deny it
But a soul that no one could
For anyone who's seen it
Wishes his was half as good.
Faith there's little small about him
Save the question of his size.
From the mountains which begat him
To the laughter in his eyes.
His sport, his love, his courage,
Preserve the sterling ring
Of the simple-minded Hillman
With the manners of a King.

Many have heard the name Gurkha but only a few have met them. Still fewer have served alongside them. Only a small number can claim the honour of their friendship and – so help me – I'm one of them.

Whenever my eye traces the Port Patrick–Cockburnspath line on the map, I'll see a thread of friendship that binds together the people of Scotland and Nepal that have worked together and protected each other for nearly two hundred years. The links and blood are still strong.

And when I recall the Southern Upland Way, it will be rolling empty hills in full summer bloom, long dark forest corridors and endless country lanes lined by leafy beech. Then I'll see the Nepalese faces calling 'Hello, hen!' the roars of laughter, my humiliation as they charged over yet another false summit and I'll understand the words about treating those two imposters, Triumph and Disaster, just the same. No one is unhappy to have finished the Way, to have DONE IT. I'll be recommending it to everyone I don't like very much, assuring them that seven days should be fine and that boots aren't really necessary. Just kidding.

Tomorrow would see us photographed for *The Scotsman*, return the van and attend the Edinburgh Military Tattoo where Kali's status would be confirmed – as the only Gurkha ever to attend clutching six items of polythene-wrapped dry cleaning while phoning all his friends so they could hear the pipes. The attendants appeared to think it almost comic that Gurkhas were in the audience and not in the show.

The Scotsman photocall (resulting in a colour picture of us all looking as grim as if we'd been suddenly laid off without compensation) showed the boys in the broad felt hats with drawn kukris. Gyan wasn't best pleased, murmuring: 'We're not supposed to draw kukris in public.' 'And who's going to stop you?' I shot back, bringing giggles from the photographer. Gyan would take a mid-day flight to sunny Southampton and the team would lose a fundamental component.

The following day, in bright early morning sunlight, Dhal, Kali and Bishwa would tap and smile on the taxi window, chorusing 'Ramro Ketiharu!' while I'd go back up to my flat and have the quietest coffee of my life.

I eventually closed The Gurkha Reiver account at the end of October (the money that continued to dribble in went thereafter straight to the Gurkha Welfare Trust). We had raised over £44,000, enough to pay a week's pension to 8,800 old soldiers. I was to receive a particularly treasured letter of thanks from George MacDonald Fraser.

Already the memories were fading. Where exactly was it that Dhal,

Gyan and I were standing in a row, discharging vast amounts of liquid nitrates over nettles, when surprised by an old Renault 4 bearing two ladies of approximately three times its vintage? 'They'll be talking about that for the rest of their lives,' I had commented. 'Which won't be long,' had added Dhal drily.

When the lads had gone I trudged into town with branded *jhola* on my back and gold crossed kukris on my lapel to deposit cash in the bank. A slim blonde stopped to say she'd read all about me. It was the actress Suzannah York in between appearances in an Edinburgh Fringe show. For once, I was speechless. She pinched my bicep, smiled and disappeared into the crowd as yours truly gulped and gawped. Recognized by film stars now – life could never improve.

But that Sunday night the Gurkha Reivers were as one. Eating together is a great bonder anyway and our achievement of 340 kilometres in eight-and-a-half days united us further. You touch such moments rarely in life. I felt complete: completely happy and completely worn out. Looking round the table, Dhal munching crackers, Kali sipping coke, with Bishwa and Gyan ripping up naan, I toasted them all in my heart, knowing I'd never meet such a bunch ever again, nor even attempt anything so rewarding. It was at this moment that Dhal turned to me and asked: 'So, Neil Sahib, what are we doing next year?'

And that is another story.

Opposite: **Cockburnspath. Mission accomplished. The beams hide fatigue; within a hour we were all asleep.**

Where are they now?

Staff Sergeant Gyan Bahadur Tamang is an instructor at the Royal School of Signals in Dorset where he lives with his wife and two sons. Gyan is due to retire and hopes to settle in the UK. He fulfilled his ambition to take his family to Paris over Easter 2003.

Corporal Dhal Bahadur Sahi is now a sergeant stationed with 250 Gurkha Signal Squadron, near Nuneaton. A piping instructor, Dhal has played his pipes all over the world, including Sweden and the USA. He, too, hopes to acquire a UK passport.

Corporal Kali Bahadur Yonghang (his clan is a sept of the Limbus) left the British Army in 2001 and is now in the Gurkha Reserve, part of the Sultan of Brunei's armed forces. He keeps in touch via a series of 1960s postcards that he bought in a job lot somewhere in Surrey.

Rifleman Bishwa Anjan Rai was promoted shortly after Gurkha Reiver to lance corporal and has served since with 2nd Battalion The Gurkha Rifles, near Folkestone. He is, I'm assured, a highly respected member of his unit.

Note: *In English a Gurkha's middle name is often written as part of the forename. This is not how Gurkhas choose to spell them and I have adopted their practice.*

What it is all about: a Himalayan hill village

Cualann Press Titles

Full Circle: Log of the Navy's No. 1 Conscript
John Gritten
Foreword: Dr Peter Liddle, Director, The Second World War Experience Centre, Leeds
ISBN 0 9535036 9 0 ... Price £19.99 (Hardback, 352 pages, illustrated)

In Search of Willie Patterson: A Scottish Soldier in the Age of Imperialism
Dr Fred Reid
Foreword: Prof W Hamish Fraser, University of Strathclyde
ISBN 0 9535036 7 4 ... Price £10.99 (p/b 160 pages, illustrated)

The Lion and the Eagle: Reminiscences of Polish Second World War Veterans in Scotland
Editor: Dr Diana M Henderson LLB TD FSA Scot.
Foreword: His Excellency Dr Stanislaw Komorowski
ISBN: 0 9535036 4 X ... £9.99 (p/b 160 pages, illustrated)

Stand By Your Beds! A Wry Look at National Service
David Findlay Clark OBE, MA, Ph.D., C.Psychol., F.B.Ps.S.
Preface: Trevor Royle, historian and writer
ISBN: 0 9535036 6 6 ... £13.99 (p/b 256 pages, illustrated)

Open Road to Faraway: Escapes from Nazi POW Camps 1941-1945
Andrew Winton D A (Edin)
Foreword: Allan Carswell, National War Museum of Scotland
ISBN: 0 9535036 5 8 ... £9.99 (p/b 160 pages, illustrated)

Beyond the Bamboo Screen: Scottish Prisoners of War under the Japanese
Tom McGowran OBE.
Foreword and Illustrations by G S Gimson QC
ISBN 0 9535036 1 5 ... Price £9.99 (p/b 160 pages, illustrated)

On Flows the Tay: Perth and the First World War
Dr Bill Harding Ph.D., FEIS
Foreword: Alan Hamilton, *The Times* journalist and author
ISBN 0 9535036 2 3 ... Price £12.99 (p/b 192 pages, illustrated)

Of Fish and Men: Tales of a Scottish Fisher
David C Watson.
Foreword: Derek Mills
ISBN 0 9535036 3 1 ... Price £10.99 (p/b 160 pages, illustrated)

Coasting around Scotland
Nicholas Fairweather
Foreword: Robin Harper MSP
ISBN 0 9535036 8 2 ... Price £12.99 (p/b 200 pages, b/w and colour photos)